FOREWORD

The collection of "Everything Will Be Okay" travel phrasebooks published by T&P Books is designed for people traveling abroad for tourism and business. The phrasebooks contain what matters most - the essentials for basic communication. This is an indispensable set of phrases to "survive" while abroad.

This phrasebook will help you in most cases where you need to ask something, get directions, find out how much something costs, etc. It can also resolve difficult communication situations where gestures just won't help.

This book contains a lot of phrases that have been grouped according to the most relevant topics. A separate section of the book also provides a small dictionary with more than 1,500 important and useful words.

Take "Everything Will Be Okay" phrasebook with you on the road and you'll have an irreplaceable traveling companion who will help you find your way out of any situation and teach you to not fear speaking with foreigners.

TABLE OF CONTENTS

T&P Books Publishing

Travel phrasebooks collection
«Everything Will Be Okay!»

T&P Books Publishing

PHRASEBOOK

— RUSSIAN —

THE MOST IMPORTANT PHRASES

This phrasebook contains
the most important
phrases and questions
for basic communication
Everything you need
to survive overseas

By Andrey Taranov

T&p BOOKS

Phrasebook + 1500-word dictionary

English-Russian phrasebook & concise dictionary

By Andrey Taranov

The collection of "Everything Will Be Okay" travel phrasebooks published by T&P Books is designed for people traveling abroad for tourism and business. The phrasebooks contain what matters most - the essentials for basic communication. This is an indispensable set of phrases to "survive" while abroad.

Another section of the book also provides a small dictionary with more than 1,500 useful words arranged alphabetically. The dictionary includes a lot of gastronomic terms and will be helpful when ordering food at a restaurant or buying groceries at the store.

Copyright © 2015 T&P Books Publishing

All rights reserved. No part of this book may be reproduced or utilized in any form or by any means, electronic or mechanical, including photocopying, recording or by information storage and retrieval system, without permission in writing from the publishers.

T&P Books Publishing
www.tpbooks.com

ISBN: 978-1-78492-431-7

This book is also available in E-book formats.
Please visit www.tpbooks.com or the major online bookstores.

PRONUNCIATION

Letter	Russian example	T&P phonetic alphabet	English example
А, а	трава	[ɑ], [a]	bath, to pass
Е, е	перерыв	[e]	elm, medal
Ё, ё	ёлка	[jɔ:], [ɜ:]	yourself, girl
И, и	филин	[i], [i:]	feet, Peter
О, о	корова	[o], [o:]	floor, doctor
У, у	Тулуза	[u], [u:]	book, shoe
Э, э	эволюция	[ɛ]	man, bad
Ю, ю	трюм	[ju:], [ju]	cued, cute
Я, я	яблоко	[ja:], [æ:]	royal
Б, б	баобаб	[b]	baby, book
В, в	врач, вино	[v]	very, river
Г, г	глагол	[g]	game, gold
Д, д	дом, труд	[d]	day, doctor
Ж, ж	живот	[ʒ]	forge, pleasure
З, з	зоопарк	[z]	zebra, please
Й, й	йога	[j]	yes, New York
ой	стройка	[ɔi]	oil, boy, point
ай	край	[aj]	time, white
К, к	кино, сок	[k]	clock, kiss
Л, л	лопата	[l]	lace, people
М, м	март, сом	[m]	magic, milk
Н, н	небо	[n]	name, normal
П, п	папа	[p]	pencil, private
Р, р	урок, робот	[r]	rice, radio
С, с	собака	[s]	city, boss
Т, т	ток, стая	[t]	tourist, trip
Ф, ф	фарфор	[f]	face, food
Х, х	хобот, страх	[h]	home, have
Ц, ц	цапля	[ts]	cats, tsetse fly
Ч, ч	чемодан	[tʃ]	church, French
Ш, ш	шум, шашки	[ʃ]	machine, shark
Щ, щ	щенок	[ɕ]	sheep, shop
Ы, ы	рыба	[ɪ]	big, America

Letter	Russian example	T&P phonetic alphabet	English example
Ь, ь	дверь	[ʲ]	soft sign - no sound
нь	конь	[ɲ]	canyon, new
ль	соль	[ʎ]	daily, million
ть	статья	[t]	tune, student
Ъ, ъ	подъезд	[ˈ]	hard sign - no sound

LIST OF ABBREVIATIONS

English abbreviations

ab.	-	about
adj	-	adjective
adv	-	adverb
anim.	-	animate
as adj	-	attributive noun used as adjective
e.g.	-	for example
etc.	-	et cetera
fam.	-	familiar
fem.	-	feminine
form.	-	formal
inanim.	-	inanimate
masc.	-	masculine
math	-	mathematics
mil.	-	military
n	-	noun
pl	-	plural
pron.	-	pronoun
sb	-	somebody
sing.	-	singular
sth	-	something
v aux	-	auxiliary verb
vi	-	intransitive verb
vi, vt	-	intransitive, transitive verb
vt	-	transitive verb

Russian abbreviations

ж	-	feminine noun
ж мн	-	feminine plural
м	-	masculine noun
м мн	-	masculine plural
м, ж	-	masculine, feminine
мн	-	plural
с	-	neuter
с мн	-	neuter plural

T&P BOOKS

RUSSIAN PHRASEBOOK

This section contains
important phrases that may
come in handy in various
real-life situations.
The phrasebook will help
you ask for directions, clarify
a price, buy tickets, and
order food at a restaurant

T&P Books Publishing

PHRASEBOOK
CONTENTS

T&P Books Publishing

The bare minimum

Excuse me, ...	**Извините, ...** [izwi'nite, ...]
Hello.	**Здравствуйте.** ['zdrastvujte]
Thank you.	**Спасибо.** [spa'sibə]
Good bye.	**До свидания.** [da swi'danija]
Yes.	**Да.** [da]
No.	**Нет.** [net]
I don't know.	**Я не знаю.** [ja ne 'znaʲʉ]
Where?	Where to?	When?	**Где?	Куда?	Когда?** [gde?	kʊ'da?	kag'da?]
I need ...	**Мне нужен ...** [mne 'nʊʒən ...]
I want ...	**Я хочу ...** [ja ha'ʧu ...]
Do you have ...?	**У вас есть ...?** [u vas estʲ ...?]
Is there a ... here?	**Здесь есть ...?** [zdesʲ estʲ ...?]
May I ...?	**Я могу ...?** [ja ma'gʊ ...?]
..., please (polite request)	**пожалуйста** [pa'ʒaləstə]
I'm looking for ...	**Я ищу ...** [ja i'ɕu ...]
restroom	**туалет** [tʊa'let]
ATM	**банкомат** [banka'mat]
pharmacy (drugstore)	**аптеку** [ap'tekʊ]
hospital	**больницу** [balʲ'nitsu]
police station	**полицейский участок** [pali'tsɛjskij u'ʧastək]
subway	**метро** [met'rɔ]

taxi	**такси** [tak'si]
train station	**вокзал** [vak'zal]

My name is ...	**Меня зовут ...** [mi'ɲa za'vʊt ...]
What's your name?	**Как вас зовут?** [kak vas za'vʊt?]
Could you please help me?	**Помогите мне, пожалуйста.** [pama'gite mne, pa'ʒaləstə]
I've got a problem.	**У меня проблема.** [u me'ɲa prab'lema]
I don't feel well.	**Мне плохо.** [mne 'plɔhə]
Call an ambulance!	**Вызовите скорую!** [vɪzawite 'skorʊʲʉ!]
May I make a call?	**Могу я позвонить?** [ma'gʊ ja pazva'nitʲ?]

I'm sorry.	**Извините.** [izwi'nite]
You're welcome.	**Пожалуйста.** [pa'ʒaləstə]

I, me	**я** [ja]
you (inform.)	**ты** [tɪ]
he	**он** [ɔn]
she	**она** [a'na]
they (masc.)	**они** [a'ni]
they (fem.)	**они** [a'ni]
we	**мы** [mɪ]
you (pl)	**вы** [vɪ]
you (sg, form.)	**Вы** [vɪ]

ENTRANCE	**ВХОД** [vhɔt]
EXIT	**ВЫХОД** ['vɪhət]
OUT OF ORDER	**НЕ РАБОТАЕТ** [ne ra'botaet]
CLOSED	**ЗАКРЫТО** [zak'rɪtə]

OPEN

ОТКРЫТО
[atk'rɪtə]

FOR WOMEN

ДЛЯ ЖЕНЩИН
[dʎa 'ʒɛnɕin]

FOR MEN

ДЛЯ МУЖЧИН
[dʎa mʊ'ɕin]

Questions

Where?	**Где?** [gde?]
Where to?	**Куда?** [kʊ'da?]
Where from?	**Откуда?** [at'kʊda?]
Why?	**Почему?** [patʃe'mʊ?]
For what reason?	**Зачем?** [za'tʃem?]
When?	**Когда?** [kag'da?]

How long?	**Как долго?** [kak 'dɔlga?]
At what time?	**Во сколько?** [va 'skɔlʲkə?]
How much?	**Сколько стоит?** ['skɔlʲkə 'stɔit?]
Do you have ...?	**У вас есть ...?** [u vas estʲ ...?]
Where is ...?	**Где находится ...?** [gde na'hɔditsa ...?]

What time is it?	**Который час?** [ka'tɔrij tʃas?]
May I make a call?	**Могу я позвонить?** [ma'gʊ ja pazva'nitʲ?]
Who's there?	**Кто там?** [ktɔ tam?]
Can I smoke here?	**Могу я здесь курить?** [ma'gʊ ja zdesʲ kʊ'ritʲ?]
May I ...?	**Я могу ...?** [ja ma'gʊ ...?]

Needs

I'd like ...
Я бы хотел /хотела/ ...
[ja bɪ ha'tel /ha'tela/ ...]

I don't want ...
Я не хочу ...
[ja ne ha'ʧu ...]

I'm thirsty.
Я хочу пить.
[ja ha'ʧu pitʲ]

I want to sleep.
Я хочу спать.
[ja ha'ʧu spatʲ]

I want ...
Я хочу ...
[ja ha'ʧu ...]

to wash up
умыться
[u'mɪtsa]

to brush my teeth
почистить зубы
[pa'ʧistitʲ 'zubɪ]

to rest a while
немного отдохнуть
[nem'nɔgə atdah'nutʲ]

to change my clothes
переодеться
[perea'detsa]

to go back to the hotel
вернуться в гостиницу
[wer'nutsa v gas'tinitsu]

to buy ...
купить ...
[ku'pitʲ ...]

to go to ...
съездить в ...
[sʰ'ezditʲ v ...]

to visit ...
посетить ...
[pasi'titʲ ...]

to meet with ...
встретиться с ...
[vstr'etitsa s ...]

to make a call
позвонить
[pazva'nitʲ]

I'm tired.
Я устал /устала/.
[ja us'tal /us'tala/]

We are tired.
Мы устали.
[mɪ us'tali]

I'm cold.
Мне холодно.
[mne 'hɔladnə]

I'm hot.
Мне жарко.
[mne 'ʒarkə]

I'm OK.
Мне нормально.
[mne nar'malʲnə]

I need to make a call.   **Мне надо позвонить.**
                              [mne 'nada pazva'nitʲ]

I need to go to the restroom. **Мне надо в туалет.**
                              [mne 'nada v tʊa'let]

I have to go.   **Мне пора.**
                              [mne pa'ra]

I have to go now.   **Мне надо идти.**
                              [mne 'nada it'ti]

Asking for directions

Excuse me, ...	**Извините, ...** [izwi'nite, ...]
Where is ...?	**Где находится ...?** [gde na'hɔditsa ...?]
Which way is ...?	**В каком направлении находится ...?** [v ka'kɔm naprav'lenii na'hɔditsa ...?]
Could you help me, please?	**Помогите мне, пожалуйста.** [pama'gite mne, pa'ʒaləstə]
I'm looking for ...	**Я ищу ...** [ja i'ɕu ...]
I'm looking for the exit.	**Я ищу выход.** [ja i'ɕu 'vɪhət]
I'm going to ...	**Я еду в ...** [ja 'edʊ v ...]
Am I going the right way to ...?	**Я правильно иду ...?** [ja 'prawilʲnə i'dʊ ...?]
Is it far?	**Это далеко?** ['ɛtə dale'kɔ?]
Can I get there on foot?	**Я дойду туда пешком?** [ja daj'dʊ tʊ'da peʃ'kɔm?]
Can you show me on the map?	**Покажите мне на карте, пожалуйста.** [paka'ʒite mne na 'karte, pa'ʒaləstə]
Show me where we are right now.	**Покажите, где мы сейчас.** [paka'ʒite, gde mɪ se'tʃas]
Here	**Здесь** [zdesʲ]
There	**Там** [tam]
This way	**Сюда** [sʲʉ'da]
Turn right.	**Поверните направо.** [pawer'nite nap'ravə]
Turn left.	**Поверните налево.** [pawer'nite na'levə]
first (second, third) turn	**первый (второй, третий) поворот** ['pervɪj (vta'rɔj, 'tretij) pava'rɔt]
to the right	**направо** [nap'ravə]

to the left   **налево**
[na'levə]

Go straight.   **Идите прямо.**
[i'dite 'prʲamə]

Signs

WELCOME!	**ДОБРО ПОЖАЛОВАТЬ!** [dab'rɔ pa'ʒalavɘtʲ!]
ENTRANCE	**ВХОД** [vhɔt]
EXIT	**ВЫХОД** ['vɪhɘt]
PUSH	**ОТ СЕБЯ** [at se'bʲa]
PULL	**НА СЕБЯ** [na se'bʲa]
OPEN	**ОТКРЫТО** [atk'rɪtɘ]
CLOSED	**ЗАКРЫТО** [zak'rɪtɘ]
FOR WOMEN	**ДЛЯ ЖЕНЩИН** [dʎa 'ʒɛnɕin]
FOR MEN	**ДЛЯ МУЖЧИН** [dʎa mʊ'ɕin]
MEN, GENTS	**МУЖСКОЙ ТУАЛЕТ** [mʊʃs'kɔj tʊa'let]
WOMEN, LADIES	**ЖЕНСКИЙ ТУАЛЕТ** [ʒɛnskij tʊa'let]
DISCOUNTS	**СКИДКИ** ['skitki]
SALE	**РАСПРОДАЖА** [raspra'daʒa]
FREE	**БЕСПЛАТНО** [bisp'latnɘ]
NEW!	**НОВИНКА!** [na'vinka!]
ATTENTION!	**ВНИМАНИЕ!** [vni'maniɘ!]
NO VACANCIES	**МЕСТ НЕТ** [mest 'net]
RESERVED	**ЗАРЕЗЕРВИРОВАНО** [zarizer'wiravanɘ]
ADMINISTRATION	**АДМИНИСТРАЦИЯ** [administ'ratsija]
STAFF ONLY	**ТОЛЬКО ДЛЯ ПЕРСОНАЛА** [tɔlʲkɘ dʎa persa'nala]

BEWARE OF THE DOG!	ЗЛАЯ СОБАКА ['zlaja sa'baka]
NO SMOKING!	НЕ КУРИТЬ! [ne kʊ'ritʲ!]
DO NOT TOUCH!	РУКАМИ НЕ ТРОГАТЬ! [rʊ'kami ne 'trɔgatʲ!]
DANGEROUS	ОПАСНО [a'pasnə]
DANGER	ОПАСНОСТЬ [a'pasnəstʲ]
HIGH VOLTAGE	ВЫСОКОЕ НАПРЯЖЕНИЕ [vɪ'sɔkae napri'ʒɛnie]
NO SWIMMING!	КУПАТЬСЯ ЗАПРЕЩЕНО [kʊ'patsa zapriɕe'nɔ!]

OUT OF ORDER	НЕ РАБОТАЕТ [ne ra'bɔtaet]
FLAMMABLE	ОГНЕОПАСНО [agnea'pasnə]
FORBIDDEN	ЗАПРЕЩЕНО [zapriɕe'nɔ]
NO TRESPASSING!	ПРОХОД ЗАПРЕЩЁН [pra'hɔt zapri'ɕʲon!]
WET PAINT	ОКРАШЕНО [ak'raʃənə]

CLOSED FOR RENOVATIONS	ЗАКРЫТО НА РЕМОНТ [zak'rɪtə na re'mɔnt]
WORKS AHEAD	РЕМОНТНЫЕ РАБОТЫ [re'mɔntnɪe ra'bɔtɪ]
DETOUR	ОБЪЕЗД [abʰ'ezt]

Transportation. General phrases

plane	**самолёт** [sama'lʲot]
train	**поезд** ['pɔest]
bus	**автобус** [aft'ɔbʊs]
ferry	**паром** [pa'rɔm]
taxi	**такси** [tak'si]
car	**машина** [ma'ʃina]
schedule	**расписание** [raspi'sanie]
Where can I see the schedule?	**Где можно посмотреть расписание?** [gde 'mɔʒnə pasmat'retʲ raspi'sanie?]
workdays (weekdays)	**рабочие дни** [ra'bɔtʃie dni]
weekends	**выходные дни** [vɪhad'nɪe dni]
holidays	**праздничные дни** ['prazdnitʃnɪe dni]
DEPARTURE	**ОТПРАВЛЕНИЕ** [atprav'lenie]
ARRIVAL	**ПРИБЫТИЕ** [pri'bɪtie]
DELAYED	**ЗАДЕРЖИВАЕТСЯ** [za'derʒivaetsa]
CANCELED	**ОТМЕНЕН** [atme'nʲon]
next (train, etc.)	**следующий** ['sledʊɕij]
first	**первый** ['pervɪj]
last	**последний** [pas'lednij]
When is the next ...?	**Когда будет следующий ...?** [kag'da 'bʊdet 'sledʊɕij ...?]
When is the first ...?	**Когда отходит первый ...?** [kag'da at'hɔdit 'pervɪj ...?]

When is the last …?

Когда уходит последний …?
[kag'da u'hɔdit pas'lednij …?]

transfer (change of trains, etc.)

пересадка
[piri'satka]

to make a transfer

сделать пересадку
['sdelatʲ piri'satkʊ]

Do I need to make a transfer?

Мне нужно делать пересадку?
[mne 'nʊʒnə 'delatʲ piri'satkʊ?]

Buying tickets

Where can I buy tickets?	**Где можно купить билеты?** [gde 'moʒnə kʊ'pitʲ bi'letɪ?]
ticket	**билет** [bi'let]
to buy a ticket	**купить билет** [kʊ'pitʲ bi'let]
ticket price	**стоимость билета** [stɔiməstʲ bi'leta]
Where to?	**Куда?** [kʊ'da?]
To what station?	**До какой станции?** [dɔ ka'kɔj 'stantsii?]
I need ...	**Мне нужно ...** [mne 'nʊʒnə ...]
one ticket	**один билет** [a'din bi'let]
two tickets	**два билета** [dva bi'leta]
three tickets	**три билета** [tri bi'leta]
one-way	**в один конец** [v a'din ka'nets]
round-trip	**туда и обратно** [tʊ'da i ab'ratnə]
first class	**первый класс** ['pervɪj klass]
second class	**второй класс** [fta'rɔj klass]
today	**сегодня** [si'vɔdɲa]
tomorrow	**завтра** ['zaftra]
the day after tomorrow	**послезавтра** [pɔsle'zaftra]
in the morning	**утром** ['utrəm]
in the afternoon	**днём** [dnʲom]
in the evening	**вечером** ['wetʃerəm]

aisle seat

место у прохода
['mestə u pra'hɔda]

window seat

место у окна
['mestə u ak'na]

How much?

Сколько?
['skɔlʲkə?]

Can I pay by credit card?

Могу я заплатить карточкой?
[ma'gu ja zapla'titʲ 'kartətʃkəj?]

Bus

bus	**автобус** [aft'ɔbʊs]
intercity bus	**междугородний автобус** [meʒdʊga'rɔdnij aft'ɔbʊs]
bus stop	**автобусная остановка** [aft'ɔbʊsnaja asta'nɔfka]
Where's the nearest bus stop?	**Где ближайшая автобусная остановка?** [gde bli'ʒajʃeja aft'ɔbʊsnaja asta'nɔfka?]

number (bus ~, etc.)	**номер** ['nɔmer]
Which bus do I take to get to …?	**Какой автобус идёт до …?** [ka'kɔj aft'ɔbʊs i'dʲot dɔ …?]
Does this bus go to …?	**Этот автобус идёт до …?** [ɛtet av'tɔbʊs i'dʲot dɔ …?]
How frequent are the buses?	**Как часто ходят автобусы?** [kak 'tʃastə 'hɔdʲat aft'ɔbʊsɪ?]

every 15 minutes	**каждые 15 минут** ['kaʒdɪe pit'natsatʲ mi'nʊt]
every half hour	**каждые полчаса** ['kaʒdɪe pɔltʃa'sa]
every hour	**каждый час** ['kaʒdɪj tʃas]
several times a day	**несколько раз в день** ['neskalʲkə raz v denʲ]
… times a day	**… раз в день** [… raz v denʲ]

schedule	**расписание** [raspi'sanie]
Where can I see the schedule?	**Где можно посмотреть расписание?** [gde 'mɔʒnə pasmat'retʲ raspi'sanie?]

When is the next bus?	**Когда будет следующий автобус?** [kag'da 'bʊdet 'sledʊɕij aft'ɔbʊs?]
When is the first bus?	**Когда отходит первый автобус?** [kag'da at'hɔdit 'pervɪj aft'ɔbʊs?]
When is the last bus?	**Когда уходит последний автобус?** [kag'da u'hɔdit pas'lednij aft'ɔbʊs?]
stop	**остановка** [asta'nɔfka]

next stop	**следующая остановка** ['sledʊɕəja asta'nɔfka]
last stop (terminus)	**конечная остановка** [ka'netʃnəja asta'nɔfka]
Stop here, please.	**Остановите здесь, пожалуйста.** [astana'wite zdesʲ, pa'ʒaləstə]
Excuse me, this is my stop.	**Разрешите, это моя остановка.** [razre'ʃite, 'ɛtə ma'ja asta'nɔfka]

Train

train	**поезд** ['poest]
suburban train	**пригородный поезд** ['prigəradnɪj 'poest]
long-distance train	**поезд дальнего следования** ['poest 'dalinevə 'sledavanija]
train station	**вокзал** [vak'zal]
Excuse me, where is the exit to the platform?	**Извините, где выход к поездам?** [izwi'nite, gde 'vɪhət k paez'dam?]

Does this train go to …?	**Этот поезд идёт до …?** [ɛtət 'poest i'diot do …?]
next train	**следующий поезд** ['sleduɕij 'poest]
When is the next train?	**Когда будет следующий поезд?** [kag'da 'budet 'sleduɕij 'poest?]
Where can I see the schedule?	**Где можно посмотреть расписание?** [gde 'moʒnə pasmat'reti raspi'sanie?]
From which platform?	**С какой платформы?** [s ka'koj plat'formɪ?]
When does the train arrive in …?	**Когда поезд прибывает в …?** [kag'da 'poest pribɪ'vaet v …?]

Please help me.	**Помогите мне, пожалуйста.** [pama'gite mne, pa'ʒaləstə]
I'm looking for my seat.	**Я ищу своё место.** [ja i'ɕu sva'io 'mestə]
We're looking for our seats.	**Мы ищем наши места.** [mɪ 'iɕem 'naʃi mes'ta]
My seat is taken.	**Моё место занято.** [ma'io 'mestə 'zaɲatə]
Our seats are taken.	**Наши места заняты.** ['naʃi mes'ta 'zaɲatɪ]

I'm sorry but this is my seat.	**Извините, пожалуйста, но это моё место.** [izwi'nite, pa'ʒaləstə, no 'ɛtə ma'io 'mestə]
Is this seat taken?	**Это место свободно?** [ɛtə 'mestə sva'bodnə?]
May I sit here?	**Могу я здесь сесть?** [ma'gu ja zdesi 'sesti?]

On the train. Dialogue (No ticket)

Ticket, please.	**Ваш билет, пожалуйста.** [vaʃ bi'let, pa'ʒaləstə]
I don't have a ticket.	**У меня нет билета.** [u me'ɲa net bi'leta]
I lost my ticket.	**Я потерял /потеряла/ свой билет.** [ja pate'rʲal /pate'rʲala/ svɔj bi'let]
I forgot my ticket at home.	**Я забыл /забыла/ билет дома.** [ja za'bɪl /za'bɪla/ bi'let 'doma]

You can buy a ticket from me.	**Вы можете купить билет у меня.** [vɪ 'mɔʒɛte ku'pitʲ bi'let u me'ɲa]
You will also have to pay a fine.	**Вам ещё придётся заплатить штраф.** [vam i'ɕо pri'dʲoʦa zapla'titʲ 'ʃtraf]
Okay.	**Хорошо.** [hara'ʃo]
Where are you going?	**Куда вы едете?** [ku'da vɪ 'edete?]
I'm going to …	**Я еду до …** [ja 'edu dɔ …]

How much? I don't understand.	**Сколько? Я не понимаю.** ['skolʲkə? ja ne pani'maʲʉ]
Write it down, please.	**Напишите, пожалуйста.** [napi'ʃite, pa'ʒaləstə]
Okay. Can I pay with a credit card?	**Хорошо. Могу я заплатить карточкой?** [hara'ʃo. ma'gu ja zapla'titʲ 'kartətʃkəj?]
Yes, you can.	**Да, можете.** [da 'mɔʒɛte]

Here's your receipt.	**Вот ваша квитанция.** [vɔt 'vaʃʌ kwi'tanʦija]
Sorry about the fine.	**Сожалею о штрафе.** [saʒə'leʲʉ ɔ 'ʃtrafe]
That's okay. It was my fault.	**Это ничего. Это моя вина.** ['ɛtə nitʃe'vo. 'ɛtə ma'ja wi'na]
Enjoy your trip.	**Приятной вам поездки.** [pri'jatnəj vam pa'eztki]

Taxi

taxi	**такси** [tak'si]
taxi driver	**таксист** [tak'sist]
to catch a taxi	**поймать такси** [paj'matʲ tak'si]
taxi stand	**стоянка такси** [sta'janka tak'si]
Where can I get a taxi?	**Где я могу взять такси?** [gde ja ma'gʊ vzʲatʲ tak'si?]
to call a taxi	**вызвать такси** ['vɪzvatʲ tak'si]
I need a taxi.	**Мне нужно такси.** [mne 'nʊʒnə tak'si]
Right now.	**Прямо сейчас.** ['prʲamə se'ʧas]
What is your address (location)?	**Ваш адрес?** [vaʃ 'adres?]
My address is ...	**Мой адрес ...** [mɔj 'adres ...]
Your destination?	**Куда вы поедете?** [kʊ'da vɪ pɔ'edete?]
Excuse me, ...	**Извините, ...** [izwi'nite, ...]
Are you available?	**Вы свободны?** [vɪ sva'bɔdnɪ?]
How much is it to get to ...?	**Сколько стоит доехать до ...?** ['skɔlʲkə 'stɔit da'ehatʲ dɔ ...?]
Do you know where it is?	**Вы знаете, где это?** [vɪ 'znaete, 'gde ɛtə?]
Airport, please.	**В аэропорт, пожалуйста.** [v aɛra'pɔrt, pa'ʒaləstə]
Stop here, please.	**Остановитесь здесь, пожалуйста.** [astana'witesʲ zdesʲ, pa'ʒaləstə]
It's not here.	**Это не здесь.** ['ɛtə ne zdesʲ]
This is the wrong address.	**Это неправильный адрес.** ['ɛtə nep'rawilʲnɪj 'adres]
Turn left.	**Сейчас налево.** [si'ʧas na'levə]
Turn right.	**Сейчас направо.** [si'ʧas nap'ravə]

How much do I owe you?

Сколько я вам должен /должна/?
['skolʲkə ja vam 'dɔlʒen /dɔlʒ'na/?]

I'd like a receipt, please.

Дайте мне чек, пожалуйста.
[dajte mne 'ʧek, pa'ʒaləstə]

Keep the change.

Сдачи не надо.
[sdatʃi ne 'nadə]

Would you please wait for me?

Подождите меня, пожалуйста.
[padaʒ'dite me'ɲa, pa'ʒaləstə]

five minutes

5 минут
[pʲatʲ mi'nʊt]

ten minutes

10 минут
['desʲatʲ mi'nʊt]

fifteen minutes

15 минут
[pit'natsatʲ mi'nʊt]

twenty minutes

20 минут
['dvatsatʲ mi'nʊt]

half an hour

полчаса
[pɔlʧa'sa]

Hotel

Hello.	**Здравствуйте.** ['zdrastvujte]
My name is …	**Меня зовут …** [mi'ɲa za'vʊt …]
I have a reservation.	**Я резервировал /резервировала/ номер.** [ja rezer'virəval /rezer'virəvala/ 'nɔmer]
I need …	**Мне нужен …** [mne 'nʊʒən …]
a single room	**одноместный номер** [ədna'mesnɪj 'nɔmer]
a double room	**двухместный номер** [dvʊh'mesnɪj 'nɔmer]
How much is that?	**Сколько он стоит?** ['skɔlʲke ɔn 'stɔit?]
That's a bit expensive.	**Это немного дорого.** [ɛtə nem'nɔgə 'dɔrəgə]
Do you have any other options?	**У вас есть еще что-нибудь?** [u vas estʲ e'ɕʲo ʃtɔ ni'bʊtʲ?]
I'll take it.	**Я возьму его.** [ja vazʲ'mʊ e'vɔ]
I'll pay in cash.	**Я заплачу наличными.** [ja zapla'ʧu na'liʧnɪmi]
I've got a problem.	**У меня проблема.** [u me'ɲa prab'lema]
My … is broken.	**Мой … сломан /Моя … сломана/** [mɔj … 'sloman /ma'ja … 'slɔmana/]
My … is out of order.	**Мой /Моя/ … не работает.** [mɔj /ma'ja/ … ne ra'bɔtaet]
TV	**телевизор (м)** [tele'wizər]
air conditioning	**кондиционер (м)** [kənditsia'ner]
tap	**кран (м)** [kran]
shower	**душ (м)** [dʊʃ]
sink	**раковина (ж)** ['rakəwina]

safe	**сейф (м)** [sɛjf]
door lock	**замок (м)** [zaˈmɔk]
electrical outlet	**розетка (ж)** [raˈzetka]
hairdryer	**фен (м)** [fen]

I don't have …	**У меня нет …** [u meˈɲa net …]
water	**воды** [vaˈdɪ]
light	**света** [ˈsweta]
electricity	**электричества** [ɛlektˈriʧestva]

Can you give me …?	**Можете мне дать …?** [ˈmɔʒete mne datʲ …?]
a towel	**полотенце** [palaˈtentse]
a blanket	**одеяло** [adeˈjalə]
slippers	**тапочки** [ˈtapəʧki]
a robe	**халат** [haˈlat]
shampoo	**шампунь** [ʃʌmˈpʊnʲ]
soap	**мыло** [ˈmɪlə]

I'd like to change rooms.	**Я хотел бы /хотела бы/ поменять номер.** [ja haˈtel /haˈtela/ bɪ pameˈɲatʲ ˈnɔmer]
I can't find my key.	**Я не могу найти свой ключ.** [ja ne maˈgʊ najˈti svɔj klʲʊʧ]
Could you open my room, please?	**Откройте мой номер, пожалуйста.** [atkˈrɔjte mɔj ˈnɔmer, paˈʒaləstə]

Who's there?	**Кто там?** [ktɔ tam?]
Come in!	**Войдите!** [vajˈdite!]
Just a minute!	**Одну минуту!** [adˈnʊ miˈnʊtʊ!]
Not right now, please.	**Пожалуйста, не сейчас.** [paˈʒaləstə, ne seˈtʃas]
Come to my room, please.	**Зайдите ко мне, пожалуйста.** [zajˈdite kam'ne, paˈʒaləstə]

I'd like to order food service.

Я хочу сделать заказ еды в номер.
[ja haˈtʃu ˈsdelatʲ zaˈkas eˈdɪ v ˈnɔmer]

My room number is ...

Мой номер комнаты ...
[mɔj ˈnɔmer ˈkɔmnatɪ ...]

I'm leaving ...

Я уезжаю ...
[ja ueˈʑʑaʲʉ ...]

We're leaving ...

Мы уезжаем ...
[mɪ ueˈʑʑaem ...]

right now

сейчас
[seˈtʃas]

this afternoon

сегодня после обеда
[seˈvɔdʲna ˈpɔsle aˈbeda]

tonight

сегодня вечером
[seˈvɔdʲna ˈwetʃerəm]

tomorrow

завтра
[ˈzaftra]

tomorrow morning

завтра утром
[ˈzaftra ˈutrəm]

tomorrow evening

завтра вечером
[ˈzaftra ˈwetʃerəm]

the day after tomorrow

послезавтра
[pɔsleˈzaftra]

I'd like to pay.

Я хотел бы /хотела бы/ рассчитаться.
[ja haˈtel /haˈtela/ bɪ rasɕiˈtatsa]

Everything was wonderful.

Всё было отлично.
[vsʲo ˈbɪlə atˈlitʃnə]

Where can I get a taxi?

Где я могу взять такси?
[gde ja maˈgʊ vzʲatʲ takˈsi?]

Would you call a taxi for me, please?

Вызовите мне такси, пожалуйста.
[vɪzawite mne takˈsi, paˈʒaləstə]

Restaurant

Can I look at the menu, please?	**Могу я посмотреть ваше меню?** [ma'gʊ ja pasmat'retʲ 'vaʃə me'nʲʉ?]
Table for one.	**Столик для одного.** [stɔlik dʎa adna'vɔ]
There are two (three, four) of us.	**Нас двое (трое, четверо).** [nas 'dvɔe ('trɔe, 'tʃetwerə)]

Smoking	**Для курящих** [dʎa kʊ'rʲaɕih]
No smoking	**Для некурящих** [dʎa nekʊ'rʲaɕih]
Excuse me! (addressing a waiter)	**Будьте добры!** ['bʊtʲte dab'rɪ!]
menu	**меню** [me'nʲʉ]
wine list	**карта вин** ['karta win]
The menu, please.	**Меню, пожалуйста.** [me'nʲʉ, pa'ʒaləstə]

Are you ready to order?	**Вы готовы сделать заказ?** [vɪ ga'tɔvɪ 'sdelatʲ za'kas?]
What will you have?	**Что вы будете заказывать?** [ʃtɔ vɪ 'bʊdete za'kazɪvatʲ?]
I'll have ...	**Я буду ...** [ja 'bʊdʊ ...]

I'm a vegetarian.	**Я вегетарианец /вегетарианка/.** [ja wegetari'anets /wegetari'anka/]
meat	**мясо** ['mʲasə]
fish	**рыба** ['rɪba]
vegetables	**овощи** ['ɔvaɕi]
Do you have vegetarian dishes?	**У вас есть вегетарианские блюда?** [u vas estʲ wegetari'anskie bʲlʲʉda?]
I don't eat pork.	**Я не ем свинину.** [ja ne 'em svi'ninʊ]
He /she/ doesn't eat meat.	**Он /она/ не ест мясо.** [an /a'na/ ne est 'mʲasə]
I am allergic to ...	**У меня аллергия на ...** [u me'ɲa aler'gija na ...]

Would you please bring me ...

Принесите мне, пожалуйста ...
[prine'site mne, pa'ʒaləstə ...]

salt | pepper | sugar

соль | перец | сахар
[sɔlʲ | 'perets | 'sahar]

coffee | tea | dessert

кофе | чай | десерт
['kofe | tʃaj | de'sert]

water | sparkling | plain

вода | с газом | без газа
[va'da | s 'gazəm | bes 'gaza]

a spoon | fork | knife

ложка | вилка | нож
['loʃka | 'wilka | nɔʃ]

a plate | napkin

тарелка | салфетка
[ta'relka | sal'fetka]

Enjoy your meal!

Приятного аппетита!
[pri'jatnəvə ape'tita!]

One more, please.

Принесите ещё, пожалуйста.
[prine'site e'ɕʲo, pa'ʒaləstə]

It was very delicious.

Было очень вкусно.
['bɪlə 'ɔtʃenʲ 'vkʊsnə]

check | change | tip

счёт | сдача | чаевые
[ɕʲot | 'sdatʃə | tʃəi'vɪe]

Check, please.
(Could I have the check, please?)

Счёт, пожалуйста.
[ɕʲot, pa'ʒaləstə]

Can I pay by credit card?

Могу я заплатить карточкой?
[ma'gʊ ja zapla'titʲ 'kartətʃkəj?]

I'm sorry, there's a mistake here.

Извините, здесь ошибка.
[izwi'nite, zdesʲ a'ʃipka]

Shopping

Can I help you?	Могу я вам помочь? [ma'gʊ ja vam pa'motʃ?]
Do you have ...?	У вас есть ...? [u vas estʲ ...?]
I'm looking for ...	Я ищу ... [ja i'ɕu ...]
I need ...	Мне нужен ... [mne 'nʊʒən ...]

I'm just looking.	Я просто смотрю. [ja 'prostə smat'rʲʉ]
We're just looking.	Мы просто смотрим. [mɪ 'prostə 'smotrim]
I'll come back later.	Я зайду позже. [ja zaj'dʊ 'poʑʑə]
We'll come back later.	Мы зайдём позже. [mɪ zaj'dʲom 'poʑʑə]
discounts	sale	скидки	распродажа ['skitki	raspra'daʒa]

Would you please show me ...	Покажите мне, пожалуйста ... [paka'ʒite mne, pa'ʒaləstə ...]
Would you please give me ...	Дайте мне, пожалуйста ... [dajte mne, pa'ʒaləstə ...]
Can I try it on?	Могу я это примерить? [ma'gʊ ja 'ɛtə pri'meritʲ?]
Excuse me, where's the fitting room?	Извините, где примерочная? [izwi'nite, gde pri'merətʃnəja?]
Which color would you like?	Какой цвет вы хотите? [ka'koj tswet vɪ ha'tite?]
size	length	размер	рост [raz'mer	rost]
How does it fit?	Подошло? [pada'ʃlo?]

How much is it?	Сколько это стоит? ['skolʲkə 'ɛtə 'stoit?]
That's too expensive.	Это слишком дорого. ['ɛtə 'sliʃkəm 'dorəgə]
I'll take it.	Я возьму это. [ja vozʲ'mʊ 'ɛtə]
Excuse me, where do I pay?	Извините, где касса? [izwi'nite, gde 'kassa?]

Will you pay in cash or credit card?

Как вы будете платить?
[kak vɪ 'budete pla'titʲ?]

In cash | with credit card

наличными | карточкой
[na'litʃnɪmi | 'kartətʃkəj]

Do you want the receipt?

Вам нужен чек?
[vam 'nuʒən tʃek?]

Yes, please.

Да, будьте добры.
[da, 'butʲte dab'rɪ]

No, it's OK.

Нет, не надо. Спасибо.
[net, ne 'nadə. spa'sibə]

Thank you. Have a nice day!

Спасибо. Всего хорошего!
[spa'sibə. vse'vɔ ha'rɔʃəvə!]

In town

Excuse me, please.	**Извините, пожалуйста …** [izwi'nite, pa'ʒalǝstǝ …]
I'm looking for …	**Я ищу …** [ja i'ɕu …]
the subway	**метро** [me'trɔ]
my hotel	**свою гостиницу** [svo^ju gas'tinitsu]
the movie theater	**кинотеатр** [kinǝte'atr]
a taxi stand	**стоянку такси** [sta'janku tak'si]
an ATM	**банкомат** [banka'mat]
a foreign exchange office	**обмен валют** [ab'men va'lʲut]
an internet café	**интернет-кафе** [intɛr'nɛt ka'fɛ]
… street	**улицу …** [ulitsu …]
this place	**вот это место** [vɔt 'ɛtǝ 'mestǝ]
Do you know where … is?	**Вы не знаете, где находится …?** [vɪ ne 'znaete, gde na'hɔditsa …?]
Which street is this?	**Как называется эта улица?** [kak nazɪ'vaetsa 'ɛta 'ulitsa?]
Show me where we are right now.	**Покажите, где мы сейчас.** [paka'ʒite, gde mɪ se'tʃas]
Can I get there on foot?	**Я дойду туда пешком?** [ja daj'du tu'da peʃ'kɔm?]
Do you have a map of the city?	**У вас есть карта города?** [u vas estʲ 'karta 'gɔrada?]
How much is a ticket to get in?	**Сколько стоит билет?** ['skolʲkǝ 'stɔit bi'let?]
Can I take pictures here?	**Здесь можно фотографировать?** [zdesʲ 'mɔʒnǝ fɔtagra'firǝvatʲ?]
Are you open?	**Вы открыты?** [vɪ atk'rɪtɪ?]

When do you open?

Во сколько вы открываетесь?
[vɔ 'skɔlʲkə vɪ atkrɪ'vaetesʲ?]

When do you close?

До которого часа вы работаете?
[dɔ ka'tɔrəvə 'ʧasa vɪ ra'bɔtaete?]

Money

money	деньги ['denⁱgi]
cash	наличные деньги [na'litʃnɪe 'denⁱgi]
paper money	бумажные деньги [bʊ'maʒnɪe 'denⁱgi]
loose change	мелочь ['melotʃ]
check | change | tip	счет | сдача | чаевые [ɕʲot | 'sdatʃə | tʃəi'vɪe]
credit card	кредитная карточка [kre'ditnəja 'kartətʃka]
wallet	бумажник [bʊ'maʒnik]
to buy	покупать [pakʊ'patⁱ]
to pay	платить [pla'titⁱ]
fine	штраф [ʃtraf]
free	бесплатно [bisp'latnə]
Where can I buy ...?	Где я могу купить ...? [gde ja ma'gʊ kʊ'pitⁱ ...?]
Is the bank open now?	Банк сейчас открыт? [bank se'tʃas atk'rɪt?]
When does it open?	Во сколько он открывается? [vɔ 'skolⁱkə ɔn atkrɪ'vaetsa?]
When does it close?	До которого часа он работает? [dɔ ka'tɔrəvə 'tʃasa an ra'bɔtaet?]
How much?	Сколько? ['skolⁱkə?]
How much is this?	Сколько это стоит? ['skolⁱkə 'ɛtə 'stɔit?]
That's too expensive.	Это слишком дорого. ['ɛtə 'sliʃkəm 'dɔragə]
Excuse me, where do I pay?	Извините, где касса? [izwi'nite, gde 'kassa?]
Check, please.	Счёт, пожалуйста. [ɕʲot, pa'ʒaləstə]

Can I pay by credit card?	**Могу я заплатить карточкой?**
	[ma'gʊ ja zapla'titʲ 'kartətʃkəj?]
Is there an ATM here?	**Здесь есть банкомат?**
	[zdesʲ estʲ banka'mat?]
I'm looking for an ATM.	**Мне нужен банкомат.**
	[mne 'nʊʒən banka'mat]

I'm looking for a foreign exchange office.	**Я ищу обмен валют.**
	[ja i'ɕu ab'men va'lʲʉt]
I'd like to change ...	**Я бы хотел /хотела/ поменять ...**
	[ja bɪ ha'tel /ha'tela/ pame'nʲatʲ ...]
What is the exchange rate?	**Какой курс обмена?**
	[ka'kɔj kʊrs ab'mena]
Do you need my passport?	**Вам нужен мой паспорт?**
	[vam 'nʊʒən mɔj 'paspərt?]

Time

What time is it?	**Который час?** [ka'tɔrij tʃas?]
When?	**Когда?** [kag'da?]
At what time?	**Во сколько?** [va 'skɔlʲkə?]
now | later | after …	**сейчас | позже | после …** [se'tʃas | 'pɔʑʑe | 'pɔsle …]
one o'clock	**Час дня** [tʃas dɲa]
one fifteen	**Час пятнадцать** [tʃas pit'natsatʲ]
one thirty	**Час тридцать** [tʃas t'rittsatʲ]
one forty-five	**Без пятнадцати два** [bez pit'natsati dva]
one | two | three	**один | два | три** [a'din | dva | tri]
four | five | six	**четыре | пять | шесть** [tʃe'tɨre | pʲatʲ | ʃestʲ]
seven | eight | nine	**семь | восемь | девять** [semʲ | 'vɔsemʲ | 'devʲatʲ]
ten | eleven | twelve	**десять | одиннадцать | двенадцать** ['desʲatʲ | a'dinnatsatʲ | dwiʲ'natsatʲ]
in …	**через …** [tʃerez …]
five minutes	**5 минут** [pʲatʲ miʲ'nʊt]
ten minutes	**10 минут** ['desʲatʲ miʲ'nʊt]
fifteen minutes	**15 минут** [pit'natsatʲ miʲ'nʊt]
twenty minutes	**20 минут** ['dvatsatʲ miʲ'nʊt]
half an hour	**полчаса** [pɔltʃa'sa]
an hour	**один час** [a'din tʃas]

in the morning	**утром** ['utrəm]
early in the morning	**рано утром** [ranə 'utrəm]
this morning	**сегодня утром** [se'vɔdɲa 'utrəm]
tomorrow morning	**завтра утром** ['zaftrə 'utrəm]
at noon	**в обед** [v a'bet]
in the afternoon	**после обеда** ['pɔsle a'beda]
in the evening	**вечером** ['wetʃerəm]
tonight	**сегодня вечером** [se'vɔdɲa 'wetʃerəm]
at night	**ночью** ['nɔtʃʲʉ]
yesterday	**вчера** [vtʃe'ra]
today	**сегодня** [si'vɔdɲa]
tomorrow	**завтра** ['zaftra]
the day after tomorrow	**послезавтра** [pɔsle'zaftra]
What day is it today?	**Какой сегодня день?** [ka'kɔj si'vɔdɲa denʲ?]
It's ...	**Сегодня ...** [se'vɔdɲa ...]
Monday	**понедельник** [pani'delʲnik]
Tuesday	**вторник** ['ftɔrnik]
Wednesday	**среда** [sri'da]
Thursday	**четверг** [tʃet'werk]
Friday	**пятница** ['pʲatnitsa]
Saturday	**суббота** [sʊ'bɔta]
Sunday	**воскресение** [vaskrə'seɲje]

Greetings. Introductions

Hello.	**Здравствуйте.** ['zdrastvʊjte]
Pleased to meet you.	**Рад /рада/ с вами познакомиться.** [rad /'rada/ s 'vami pazna'komitsa]
Me too.	**Я тоже.** [ja 'toʒɛ]
I'd like you to meet …	**Знакомьтесь. Это …** [zna'komⁱtesⁱ. 'ɛtə …]
Nice to meet you.	**Очень приятно.** [otʃenⁱ pri'jatnə]
How are you?	**Как вы? | Как у вас дела?** [kak vɪ? | kak u vas de'la?]
My name is …	**Меня зовут …** [mi'ɲa za'vʊt …]
His name is …	**Его зовут …** [e'vɔ za'vʊt …]
Her name is …	**Её зовут …** [eⁱo za'vʊt …]
What's your name?	**Как вас зовут?** [kak vas za'vʊt?]
What's his name?	**Как его зовут?** [kak e'vɔ za'vʊt?]
What's her name?	**Как ее зовут?** [kak eⁱo za'vʊt?]
What's your last name?	**Как ваша фамилия?** [kak 'vaʃʌ fa'milija?]
You can call me …	**Зовите меня …** [za'wite me'ɲa …]
Where are you from?	**Откуда вы?** [at'kʊda vɪ]
I'm from …	**Я из …** [ja iz …]
What do you do for a living?	**Кем вы работаете?** [kem vɪ ra'botaete?]
Who is this?	**Кто это?** [ktɔ 'ɛtə?]
Who is he?	**Кто он?** [ktɔ ɔn?]
Who is she?	**Кто она?** [ktɔ a'na?]
Who are they?	**Кто они?** [ktɔ a'ni?]

This is …	**Это …** ['ɛtə …]
my friend (masc.)	**мой друг** [mɔj drʊk]
my friend (fem.)	**моя подруга** [ma'ja pad'rʊga]
my husband	**мой муж** [mɔj mʊʃ]
my wife	**моя жена** [ma'ja ʒi'na]

my father	**мой отец** [mɔj a'tets]
my mother	**моя мама** [ma'ja 'mama]
my brother	**мой брат** [mɔj brat]
my sister	**моя сестра** [ma'ja sist'ra]
my son	**мой сын** [mɔj sɪn]
my daughter	**моя дочь** [ma'ja dotʃ]

This is our son.	**Это наш сын.** ['ɛtə naʃ sɪn]
This is our daughter.	**Это наша дочь.** ['ɛtə 'naʃʌ dotʃ]
These are my children.	**Это мои дети.** ['ɛtə ma'i 'deti]
These are our children.	**Это наши дети.** ['ɛtə 'naʃi 'deti]

Farewells

Good bye!	**До свидания!** [dɔ swi'danija!]
Bye! (inform.)	**Пока!** [pa'ka!]
See you tomorrow.	**До завтра.** [dɔ 'zaftra]
See you soon.	**До встречи.** [dɔ vstr'etʃi]
See you at seven.	**Встретимся в семь.** [vstr'etimsʲa v semʲ]
Have fun!	**Развлекайтесь!** [razvle'kajtesʲ!]
Talk to you later.	**Поговорим попозже.** [pagava'rim pa'pɔʑʑə]
Have a nice weekend.	**Удачных выходных.** [u'datʃnɨh vɨhad'nɨh]
Good night.	**Спокойной ночи.** [spa'kɔjnej 'nɔtʃi]
It's time for me to go.	**Мне пора.** [mne pa'ra]
I have to go.	**Мне надо идти.** [mne 'nadə it'ti]
I will be right back.	**Я сейчас вернусь.** [ja se'tʃas wer'nusʲ]
It's late.	**Уже поздно.** [u'ʒɛ 'pɔzdnə]
I have to get up early.	**Мне рано вставать.** [mne 'ranə vsta'vatʲ]
I'm leaving tomorrow.	**Я завтра уезжаю.** [ja 'zaftra ue'ʑʑaʉ]
We're leaving tomorrow.	**Мы завтра уезжаем.** [mɨ 'zaftra ue'ʑʑaem]
Have a nice trip!	**Счастливой поездки!** [ɕas'livej pa'eztki!]
It was nice meeting you.	**Было приятно с вами познакомиться.** ['bɨlə pri'jatnə s 'vami pazna'kɔmitsa]
It was nice talking to you.	**Было приятно с вами пообщаться.** ['bɨlə pri'jatnə s 'vami paab'ɕatsa]

Thanks for everything.

Спасибо за всё.
[spa'sibə za 'vsʲo]

I had a very good time.

Я прекрасно провёл /провела/ время.
[ja pre'krasnə pra'wʲol /prawe'la/ 'vremʲa]

We had a very good time.

Мы прекрасно провели время.
[mɪ pre'krasnə prawe'li 'vremʲa]

It was really great.

Всё было замечательно.
[vsʲo 'bɪlə zame'tʃatelʲnə]

I'm going to miss you.

Я буду скучать.
[ja 'bʊdʊ skʊ'tʃatʲ]

We're going to miss you.

Мы будем скучать.
[mɪ 'bʊdem skʊ'tʃatʲ]

Good luck!

Удачи! Счастливо!
[u'datʃi! 'çaslive!]

Say hi to …

Передавайте привет …
[pereda'vajte pri'wet …]

Foreign language

I don't understand.	**Я не понимаю.** [ja ne pani'maʲʉ]
Write it down, please.	**Напишите это, пожалуйста.** [napi'ʃite 'ɛtə, pa'ʒaləstə]
Do you speak ...?	**Вы знаете ...?** [vɪ 'znaete ...?]

I speak a little bit of ...	**Я немного знаю ...** [ja nem'nɔgə 'znaʲʉ ...]
English	**английский** [ang'lijskij]
Turkish	**турецкий** [tʊ'reʦkij]
Arabic	**арабский** [a'rapskij]
French	**французский** [fran'ʦuskij]

German	**немецкий** [ne'meʦkij]
Italian	**итальянский** [ita'ljanskij]
Spanish	**испанский** [is'panskij]
Portuguese	**португальский** [partʊgalʲskij]
Chinese	**китайский** [ki'tajskij]
Japanese	**японский** [ja'pɔnskij]

Can you repeat that, please.	**Повторите, пожалуйста.** [pavta'rite, pa'ʒaləstə]
I understand.	**Я понимаю.** [ja pani'maʲʉ]
I don't understand.	**Я не понимаю.** [ja ne pani'maʲʉ]
Please speak more slowly.	**Говорите медленнее, пожалуйста.** [gava'rite 'medlenee, pa'ʒaləstə]

Is that correct? (Am I saying it right?)	**Это правильно?** ['ɛtə 'prawilʲnə?]
What is this? (What does this mean?)	**Что это?** [ʃtɔ 'ɛtə?]

Apologies

Excuse me, please.	**Извините, пожалуйста.** [izwi'nite, pa'ʒaləstə]
I'm sorry.	**Я сожалею.** [ja saʒə'leʲʉ]
I'm really sorry.	**Мне очень жаль.** [mne 'ɔtʃenʲ ʒalʲ]
Sorry, it's my fault.	**Виноват /Виновата/, это моя вина.** [wina'vat /wina'vata/, 'ɛtə ma'ja wi'na]
My mistake.	**Моя ошибка.** [ma'ja a'ʃipka]
May I ...?	**Могу я ...?** [ma'gʊ ja ...?]
Do you mind if I ...?	**Вы не будете возражать, если я ...?** [vɪ ne 'bʊdete vazra'ʒatʲ, 'esli ja ...?]
It's OK.	**Ничего страшного.** [nitʃe'vɔ 'straʃnəvə]
It's all right.	**Всё в порядке.** [vsʲo v pa'rʲatke]
Don't worry about it.	**Не беспокойтесь.** [ne bespa'kɔjtesʲ]

Agreement

Yes.	**Да.** [da]
Yes, sure.	**Да, конечно.** [da, ka'neʃnə]
OK (Good!)	**Хорошо!** [hara'ʃo!]
Very well.	**Очень хорошо.** ['ɔtʃenʲ hara'ʃo]
Certainly!	**Конечно!** [ka'neʃnə!]
I agree.	**Я согласен /согласна/.** [ja sag'lasen /sag'lasna/]
That's correct.	**Верно.** ['wernə]
That's right.	**Правильно.** ['prawilʲnə]
You're right.	**Вы правы.** [vɪ 'pravɪ]
I don't mind.	**Я не возражаю.** [ja ne vazra'ʒaʲʉ]
Absolutely right.	**Совершенно верно.** [sawer'ʃɛnnə 'wernə]
It's possible.	**Это возможно.** ['ɛtə vaz'mɔʒnə]
That's a good idea.	**Это хорошая мысль.** [ɛtə ha'rɔʃəja mɪslʲ]
I can't say no.	**Не могу отказать.** [ne ma'gʊ atka'zatʲ]
I'd be happy to.	**Буду рад /рада/.** [bʊdʊ rad /'rada/]
With pleasure.	**С удовольствием.** [s uda'vɔlʲstwiem]

Refusal. Expressing doubt

No.
Нет.
[net]

Certainly not.
Конечно нет.
[ka'neʃnə net]

I don't agree.
Я не согласен /не согласна/.
[ja ne sag'lasen /ne sag'lasna/]

I don't think so.
Я так не думаю.
[ja tak ne 'dʊmaʲʉ]

It's not true.
Это неправда.
['ɛtə nep'ravda]

You are wrong.
Вы неправы.
[vɪ nep'ravɪ]

I think you are wrong.
Я думаю, что вы неправы.
[ja 'dʊmaʲʉ, ʃtɔ vɪ nep'ravɪ]

I'm not sure.
Не уверен /не уверена/.
[ne u'veren /ne u'verena/]

It's impossible.
Это невозможно.
['ɛtə nevaz'mɔʒnə]

Nothing of the kind (sort)!
Ничего подобного!
[niʧe'vɔ pa'dɔbnəvə!]

The exact opposite.
Наоборот!
[naaba'rɔt!]

I'm against it.
Я против.
[ja 'prɔtiv]

I don't care.
Мне всё равно.
[mne vsʲo rav'nɔ]

I have no idea.
Понятия не имею.
[pa'ɲatija ne i'meʲʉ]

I doubt that.
Сомневаюсь, что это так.
[samne'vaʲʉsʲ, ʃtɔ 'ɛtə tak]

Sorry, I can't.
Извините, я не могу.
[izwi'nite, ja ne ma'gʊ]

Sorry, I don't want to.
Извините, я не хочу.
[izwi'nite, ja ne ha'ʧu]

Thank you, but I don't need this.
Спасибо, мне это не нужно.
[spa'sibə, mne 'ɛtə ne 'nʊʒnə]

It's late.
Уже поздно.
[u'ʒɛ 'pɔzdnə]

I have to get up early.

Мне рано вставать.
[mne 'ranə vsta'vatʲ]

I don't feel well.

Я плохо себя чувствую.
[ja 'plɔhə se'bʲa 'ʧustvʊʲʉ]

Expressing gratitude

Thank you.	**Спасибо.** [spa'sibə]
Thank you very much.	**Спасибо большое.** [spa'sibə bal^j'ʃoe]
I really appreciate it.	**Очень признателен /признательна/.** [ɔtʃenʲ priz'natelen /priz'natelʲna/]
I'm really grateful to you.	**Я вам благодарен /благодарна/.** [ja vam blaga'daren /blaga'darna/]
We are really grateful to you.	**Мы Вам благодарны.** [mɪ vam blaga'darnɪ]
Thank you for your time.	**Спасибо, что потратили время.** [spa'sibə, ʃtɔ pat'ratili 'vremʲa]
Thanks for everything.	**Спасибо за всё.** [spa'sibə za 'vsʲo]
Thank you for …	**Спасибо за …** [spa'sibə za …]
your help	**вашу помощь** [vaʃʊ 'pɔmaɕ]
a nice time	**хорошее время** [ha'rɔʃee 'vremʲa]
a wonderful meal	**прекрасную еду** [pre'krasnʊʲʉ e'dʊ]
a pleasant evening	**приятный вечер** [pri'jatnɪj 'wetʃer]
a wonderful day	**замечательный день** [zami'ʧatelʲnɪj denʲ]
an amazing journey	**интересную экскурсию** [inte'resnʊʲʉ ɛks'kʊrsiʲʉ]
Don't mention it.	**Не за что.** [ne za ʃtə]
You are welcome.	**Не стоит благодарности.** [ne 'stɔit blaga'darnasti]
Any time.	**Всегда пожалуйста.** [vseg'da pa'ʒaləsta]
My pleasure.	**Был рад /Была рада/ помочь.** [bɪl rad /bɪ'la 'rada/ pa'mɔtʃ]
Forget it. It's alright.	**Забудьте. Всё в порядке.** [za'butʲte. fsʲo f pɔ'rʲatke]
Don't worry about it.	**Не беспокойтесь.** [ne bespa'kɔjtesʲ]

Congratulations. Best wishes

Congratulations!
Поздравляю!
[pazdrav'ʎaʲʉ!]

Happy birthday!
С днём рождения!
[s 'dnʲom raʒ'denija!]

Merry Christmas!
Весёлого рождества!
[we'sʲoləvə raʒdest'va!]

Happy New Year!
С Новым годом!
[s 'nɔvɪm 'gɔdəm!]

Happy Easter!
Со Светлой Пасхой!
[sɔ 'swetləj 'pashəj!]

Happy Hanukkah!
Счастливой Хануки!
[ças'livəj 'hanʊki!]

I'd like to propose a toast.
У меня есть тост.
[u me'ɲa estʲ tɔst]

Cheers!
За ваше здоровье!
[za 'vaʃə zda'rɔvje]

Let's drink to ...!
Выпьем за ... !
['vɪpjem za ... !]

To our success!
За наш успех!
[za naʃ us'peh!]

To your success!
За ваш успех!
[za vaʃ us'peh!]

Good luck!
Удачи!
[u'datʃi!]

Have a nice day!
Приятного вам дня!
[pri'jatnəvə vam dɲa!]

Have a good holiday!
Хорошего вам отдыха!
[ha'rɔʃəvə vam 'ɔtdɪha!]

Have a safe journey!
Удачной поездки!
[u'datʃnəj pa'eztki!]

I hope you get better soon!
Желаю вам скорого выздоровления!
[ʒe'laʲʉ vam 'skɔrəvə vɪzdarav'lenija!]

Socializing

Why are you sad?	**Почему вы расстроены?** [patʃe'mʊ vɪ rast'rɔenɪ?]
Smile! Cheer up!	**Улыбнитесь!** [ulɪb'nitesʲl]
Are you free tonight?	**Вы не заняты сегодня вечером?** [vɪ ne zaɲatɪ se'vɔdɲa 'wetʃerəm?]
May I offer you a drink?	**Могу я предложить вам выпить?** [ma'gʊ ja predla'ʒitʲ vam 'vɪpitʲ?]
Would you like to dance?	**Не хотите потанцевать?** [ne ha'tite patantse'vatʲ?]
Let's go to the movies.	**Может сходим в кино?** ['mɔʒet 'shɔdim v ki'nɔ?]
May I invite you to ...?	**Могу я пригласить вас в ...?** [ma'gʊ ja prigla'sitʲ vas v ...?]
a restaurant	**ресторан** [resta'ran]
the movies	**кино** [ki'nɔ]
the theater	**театр** [te'atr]
go for a walk	**на прогулку** [na pra'gʊlkʊ]
At what time?	**Во сколько?** [va 'skɔlʲkə?]
tonight	**сегодня вечером** [se'vɔdɲa 'wetʃerəm]
at six	**в 6 часов** [v ʃɛstʲ tʃa'sɔf]
at seven	**в 7 часов** [v semʲ tʃa'sɔf]
at eight	**в 8 часов** [v 'vɔsemʲ tʃa'sɔf]
at nine	**в 9 часов** [v 'devʲatʲ tʃa'sɔf]
Do you like it here?	**Вам здесь нравится?** [vam zdesʲ 'nrawitsa?]
Are you here with someone?	**Вы здесь с кем-то?** [vɪ zdesʲ s 'kem tə?]
I'm with my friend.	**Я с другом /подругой/.** [ja s 'drʊgəm /pad'rʊgəj/]

I'm with my friends.
Я с друзьями.
[ja s drʊ'zjʲami]

No, I'm alone.
Я один /одна/.
[ja a'din /ad'na/]

Do you have a boyfriend?
У тебя есть приятель?
[u te'bʲa estʲ prʲi'jatelʲ?]

I have a boyfriend.
У меня есть друг.
[u me'ɲa estʲ drʊk]

Do you have a girlfriend?
У тебя есть подружка?
[u te'bʲa estʲ pad'rʊʃka?]

I have a girlfriend.
У меня есть девушка.
[u me'ɲa estʲ 'devʊʃka]

Can I see you again?
Мы еще встретимся?
[mɪ e'ɕʲo vst'retimsʲa?]

Can I call you?
Можно я тебе позвоню?
[mɔʒnə ja te'be pazva'nʲʉ?]

Call me. (Give me a call.)
Позвони мне.
[pazva'ni mne]

What's your number?
Какой у тебя номер?
[ka'kɔj u te'bʲa 'nɔmer?]

I miss you.
Я скучаю по тебе.
[ja skʊ'tʃaʲʉ pa te'be]

You have a beautiful name.
У вас очень красивое имя.
[u vas 'ɔtʃenʲ kra'sivae 'imʲa]

I love you.
Я тебя люблю.
[ja te'bʲa lʲʉb'lʲʉ]

Will you marry me?
Выходи за меня.
[vɪha'di za me'ɲa]

You're kidding!
Вы шутите!
[vɪ 'ʃʊtite!]

I'm just kidding.
Я просто шучу.
[ja 'prɔstə ʃʊ'tʃu]

Are you serious?
Вы серьезно?
[vɪ se'rʲoznə?]

I'm serious.
Я серьёзно.
[ja se'rʲoznə]

Really?!
Правда?!
['pravda?!]

It's unbelievable!
Это невероятно!
['ɛtə newera'jatnə]

I don't believe you.
Я вам не верю.
[ja vam ne 'werʲʉ]

I can't.
Я не могу.
[ja ne ma'gʊ]

I don't know.
Я не знаю.
[ja ne 'znaʲʉ]

I don't understand you.
Я вас не понимаю.
[ja vas ne pani'maʲʉ]

Please go away.

Уйдите, пожалуйста.
[uj'dite, pa'ʒaləstə]

Leave me alone!

Оставьте меня в покое!
[as'tavʲte meˈɲa v paˈkɔe!]

I can't stand him.

Я его не выношу.
[ja eˈgɔ ne vɪnaˈʃʊ]

You are disgusting!

Вы отвратительны!
[vɪ atvraˈtitelʲnɪ!]

I'll call the police!

Я вызову полицию!
[ja ˈvɪzavʊ paˈliʦiʲʉ!]

Sharing impressions. Emotions

I like it.	**Мне это нравится.** [mne 'ɛtə 'nrawiʦa]
Very nice.	**Очень мило.** ['ɔʧenʲ 'milə]
That's great!	**Это здорово!** ['ɛtə 'zdɔrɔvə!]
It's not bad.	**Это неплохо.** ['ɛtə nep'lɔhə]
I don't like it.	**Мне это не нравится.** [mne 'ɛtə ne 'nrawiʦa]
It's not good.	**Это нехорошо.** ['ɛtə nehara'ʃɔ]
It's bad.	**Это плохо.** ['ɛtə 'plɔhə]
It's very bad.	**Это очень плохо.** ['ɛtə 'ɔʧenʲ 'plɔhə]
It's disgusting.	**Это отвратительно.** ['ɛtə atvra'titelʲnə]
I'm happy.	**Я счастлив /счастлива/.** [ja 'ɕʲasliv /'ɕʲasliva/]
I'm content.	**Я доволен /довольна/.** [ja da'vɔlen /da'vɔlʲna/]
I'm in love.	**Я влюблён /влюблена/.** [ja vlʲʉb'lʲon /vlʲʉble'na/]
I'm calm.	**Я спокоен /спокойна/.** [ja spa'kɔen /spa'kɔjna/]
I'm bored.	**Мне скучно.** [mne 'skuʃnə]
I'm tired.	**Я устал /устала/.** [ja us'tal /us'tala/]
I'm sad.	**Мне грустно.** [mne 'grusnə]
I'm frightened.	**Я напуган /напугана/.** [ja na'pʊgan /na'pʊgana/]
I'm angry.	**Я злюсь.** [ja zlʲʉsʲ]
I'm worried.	**Я волнуюсь.** [ja val'nʊʲʉsʲ]
I'm nervous.	**Я нервничаю.** [ja 'nervniʧaʲʉ]

I'm jealous. (envious)   **Я завидую.**
[ja zaˈwiduʲʉ]

I'm surprised.   **Я удивлён /удивлена/.**
[ja udivˈlʲon /udivleˈna/]

I'm perplexed.   **Я озадачен /озадачена/.**
[ja azaˈdatʃen /azaˈdatʃena/]

Problems. Accidents

I've got a problem.	**У меня проблема.** [u me'ɲa prab'lema]
We've got a problem.	**У нас проблема.** [u nas prab'lema]
I'm lost.	**Я заблудился /заблудилась/.** [ja zablu'dilsʲa /zablu'dilasʲ/]
I missed the last bus (train).	**Я опоздал на последний автобус (поезд).** [ja apaz'dal na pas'lednij aft'ɔbʊs ('pɔest)]
I don't have any money left.	**У меня совсем не осталось денег.** [u me'ɲa sav'sem ne as'taləsʲ 'denek]

I've lost my ...	**Я потерял /потеряла/ ...** [ja pate'rʲal /pate'rʲala/ ...]
Someone stole my ...	**У меня украли ...** [u me'ɲa uk'rali ...]
passport	**паспорт** ['paspərt]
wallet	**бумажник** [bʊ'maʒnik]
papers	**документы** [dakʊ'mentɪ]
ticket	**билет** [bi'let]

money	**деньги** ['denʲgi]
handbag	**сумку** ['sʊmkʊ]
camera	**фотоаппарат** ['fɔta apa'rat]
laptop	**ноутбук** [nɔut'bʊk]
tablet computer	**планшет** [plan'ʃət]
mobile phone	**телефон** [tele'fɔn]

Help me!	**Помогите!** [pama'gite]
What's happened?	**Что случилось?** [ʃtɔ slu'ʧiləsʲ?]

fire	**пожар** [pa'ʒar]
shooting	**стрельба** [strelʲ'ba]
murder	**убийство** [u'bijstvə]
explosion	**взрыв** [vzrɪv]
fight	**драка** ['draka]

Call the police!	**Вызовите полицию!** ['vɪzawite pa'litsiʲʉ!]
Please hurry up!	**Пожалуйста, быстрее!** [pa'ʒaləstə, bɪst'ree!]
I'm looking for the police station.	**Я ищу полицейский участок.** [ja i'ɕu pali'tsɛjskij u'ʧastək]
I need to make a call.	**Мне нужно позвонить.** [mne 'nʊʒnə pazva'nitʲ]
May I use your phone?	**Могу я позвонить?** [ma'gʊ ja pazva'nitʲ?]

I've been ...	**Меня ...** [mi'ɲa ...]
mugged	**ограбили** [ag'rabili]
robbed	**обокрали** [abak'rali]
raped	**изнасиловали** [izna'siləvali]
attacked (beaten up)	**избили** [iz'bili]

Are you all right?	**С вами все в порядке?** [s 'vami vsʲo v pa'rʲatke?]
Did you see who it was?	**Вы видели, кто это был?** [vɪ 'wideli, ktɔ 'ɛtə bɪl?]
Would you be able to recognize the person?	**Вы сможете его узнать?** [vɪ s'mɔʒete e'vɔ uz'natʲ?]
Are you sure?	**Вы точно уверены?** [vɪ 'tɔʧnə u'werenɪ?]

Please calm down.	**Пожалуйста, успокойтесь.** [pa'ʒaləstə, uspa'kɔjtesʲ]
Take it easy!	**Спокойнее!** [spa'kɔjnee!]
Don't worry!	**Не беспокойтесь.** [ne bespa'kɔjtesʲ]
Everything will be fine.	**Всё будет хорошо.** [vsʲo 'bʊdet hara'ʃɔ]
Everything's all right.	**Всё в порядке.** [vsʲo v pa'rʲatke]

Come here, please.
Подойдите, пожалуйста.
[pɐdaj'dite, pa'ʒaləstə]

I have some questions for you.
У меня к вам несколько вопросов.
[u me'ɲa k vam 'neskalʲkə vap'rɔsəf]

Wait a moment, please.
Подождите, пожалуйста.
[padaʒ'dite, pa'ʒaləstə]

Do you have any I.D.?
У вас есть документы?
[u vas estʲ dakʊ'mentɪ?]

Thanks. You can leave now.
Спасибо. Вы можете идти.
[spa'sibə. vɪ 'mɔʒɛte it'ti]

Hands behind your head!
Руки за голову!
['rʊki 'zagalavʊ!]

You're under arrest!
Вы арестованы!
[vɪ ares'tɔvanɪ!]

Health problems

Please help me.	**Помогите, пожалуйста.** [pama'gite, pa'ʒaləstə]
I don't feel well.	**Мне плохо.** [mne 'plɔhə]
My husband doesn't feel well.	**Моему мужу плохо.** [mae'mʊ 'mʊʒu 'plɔhə]
My son ...	**Моему сыну ...** [mae'mʊ 'sɪnʊ ...]
My father ...	**Моему отцу ...** [mae'mʊ at'tsu ...]
My wife doesn't feel well.	**Моей жене плохо.** [ma'ej ʒɛne 'plɔhə]
My daughter ...	**Моей дочери ...** [ma'ej 'dɔtʃeri ...]
My mother ...	**Моей матери ...** [ma'ej 'materi ...]
I've got a ...	**У меня болит ...** [u me'ɲa ba'lit ...]
headache	**голова** [gala'va]
sore throat	**горло** ['gɔrlə]
stomach ache	**живот** [ʒɪ'vɔt]
toothache	**зуб** [zup]
I feel dizzy.	**У меня кружится голова.** [u me'ɲa krʊʒitsa gala'va]
He has a fever.	**У него температура.** [u ne'vɔ tempera'tʊra]
She has a fever.	**У неё температура.** [u ne'ɵ tempera'tʊra]
I can't breathe.	**Я не могу дышать.** [ja ne ma'gʊ dɪ'ʃʌtʲ]
I'm short of breath.	**Я задыхаюсь.** [ja zadɪ'haʲusʲ]
I am asthmatic.	**Я астматик.** [ja ast'matik]
I am diabetic.	**Я диабетик.** [ja dia'betik]

| I can't sleep. | **У меня бессонница.**
[u me'ɲa bes'sɔnitsa] |
| food poisoning | **пищевое отравление**
[piɕe'vɔe atrav'lenie] |

It hurts here.	**Болит вот здесь.** [ba'lit vɔt zdesʲ]
Help me!	**Помогите!** [pama'gite!]
I am here!	**Я здесь!** [ja zdesʲ!]
We are here!	**Мы здесь!** [mɪ zdesʲ!]
Get me out of here!	**Вытащите меня!** ['vɪtaɕite me'ɲa!]
I need a doctor.	**Мне нужен врач.** [mne 'nuʒen vratʃ]
I can't move.	**Я не могу двигаться.** [ja ne ma'gu 'dvigatsa]
I can't move my legs.	**Я не чувствую ног.** [ja ne 'tʃustvuʲʉ nɔk]

I have a wound.	**Я ранен /ранена/.** [ja 'ranen /'ranena/]
Is it serious?	**Это серьезно?** ['ɛtə se'rʲʲoznə?]
My documents are in my pocket.	**Мои документы в кармане.** [ma'i daku'mentɪ v kar'mane]
Calm down!	**Успокойтесь!** [uspa'kɔjtesʲ!]
May I use your phone?	**Могу я позвонить?** [ma'gu ja pazva'nitʲ?]

Call an ambulance!	**Вызовите скорую!** [vɪzawite 'skɔruʲʉ!]
It's urgent!	**Это срочно!** ['ɛtə 'srɔtʃnə!]
It's an emergency!	**Это очень срочно!** ['ɛtə 'ɔtʃenʲ 'srɔtʃnə!]
Please hurry up!	**Пожалуйста, быстрее!** [pa'ʒaləstə, bɪst'ree!]
Would you please call a doctor?	**Вызовите врача, пожалуйста.** [vɪzawite vra'tʃa, pa'ʒaləstə]
Where is the hospital?	**Скажите, где больница?** [ska'ʒite, gde balʲ'nitsa?]

How are you feeling?	**Как вы себя чувствуете?** [kak vɪ se'bʲa 'tʃustvuete?]
Are you all right?	**С вами все в порядке?** [s 'vami vsʲo v pa'rʲatke?]
What's happened?	**Что случилось?** [ʃtɔ slu'tʃiləsʲ?]

I feel better now.

Мне уже лучше.
[mne u'ʒe 'lutʃɛ]

It's OK.

Всё в порядке.
[vsʲo v paˈrʲatke]

It's all right.

Всё хорошо.
[vsʲo haraˈʃɔ]

At the pharmacy

pharmacy (drugstore)

Аптека
[ap'teka]

24-hour pharmacy

круглосуточная аптека
[krʊgla'sʊtətʃnəja ap'teka]

Where is the closest pharmacy?

Где ближайшая аптека?
[gde bli'ʒajʃəja ap'teka?]

Is it open now?

Она сейчас открыта?
[a'na se'tʃas atk'rɪta?]

At what time does it open?

Во сколько она открывается?
[va 'skolʲkə a'na atkrɪ'vaetsa?]

At what time does it close?

До которого часа она работает?
[dɔ ka'tɔrəvə 'tʃasa a'na ra'bɔtaet?]

Is it far?

Это далеко?
['ɛtə dale'kɔ?]

Can I get there on foot?

Я дойду туда пешком?
[ja daj'dʊ tʊ'da peʃ'kɔm?]

Can you show me on the map?

Покажите мне на карте, пожалуйста.
[paka'ʒite mne na 'karte, pa'ʒaləstə]

Please give me something for ...

Дайте мне, что-нибудь от ...
['dajte mne, ʃtɔ ni'bʊtʲ ɔt ...]

a headache

головной боли
[galav'nɔj 'bɔli]

a cough

кашля
['kaʃʎa]

a cold

простуды
[pras'tʊdɪ]

the flu

гриппа
['gripa]

a fever

температуры
[tempera'tʊrɪ]

a stomach ache

боли в желудке
['bɔli v ʒi'lutke]

nausea

тошноты
[taʃna'tɪ]

diarrhea

диареи
[dia'rei]

constipation

запора
[za'pɔra]

pain in the back

боль в спине
[bɔlʲ v spi'ne]

chest pain	**боль в груди**
	['bolʲ v grʊ'di]
side stitch	**боль в боку**
	[bolʲ v ba'kʊ]
abdominal pain	**боль в животе**
	['bolʲ v ʒiva'te]

pill	**таблетка**
	[tab'letka]
ointment, cream	**мазь, крем**
	[mazʲ, krem]
syrup	**сироп**
	[si'rɔp]
spray	**спрей**
	[sprɛj]
drops	**капли**
	['kapli]

You need to go to the hospital.	**Вам нужно в больницу.**
	[vam 'nʊʒnə v balʲ'nitsu]
health insurance	**страховка**
	[stra'hɔvka]
prescription	**рецепт**
	[re'ʦept]
insect repellant	**средство от насекомых**
	['sredstvə at nase'kɔmɪh]
Band Aid	**лейкопластырь**
	[lejkə'plastɪrʲ]

The bare minimum

Excuse me, ...	**Извините, ...** [izwi'nite, ...]
Hello.	**Здравствуйте.** ['zdrastvujte]
Thank you.	**Спасибо.** [spa'sibə]
Good bye.	**До свидания.** [da swi'danija]
Yes.	**Да.** [da]
No.	**Нет.** [net]
I don't know.	**Я не знаю.** [ja ne 'znaʲʉ]
Where?	Where to?	When?	**Где?	Куда?	Когда?** [gde?	kʊ'da?	kag'da?]
I need ...	**Мне нужен ...** [mne 'nʊʒən ...]
I want ...	**Я хочу ...** [ja ha'ʧu ...]
Do you have ...?	**У вас есть ...?** [u vas estʲ ...?]
Is there a ... here?	**Здесь есть ...?** [zdesʲ estʲ ...?]
May I ...?	**Я могу ...?** [ja ma'gʊ ...?]
..., please (polite request)	**пожалуйста** [pa'ʒaləstə]
I'm looking for ...	**Я ищу ...** [ja i'ɕu ...]
restroom	**туалет** [tʊa'let]
ATM	**банкомат** [banka'mat]
pharmacy (drugstore)	**аптеку** [ap'tekʊ]
hospital	**больницу** [balʲ'nitsu]
police station	**полицейский участок** [pali'tsɛjskij u'ʧastək]
subway	**метро** [met'rɔ]

taxi	**такси** [tak'si]
train station	**вокзал** [vak'zal]

My name is ...	**Меня зовут ...** [mi'ɲa za'vʊt ...]
What's your name?	**Как вас зовут?** [kak vas za'vʊt?]
Could you please help me?	**Помогите мне, пожалуйста.** [pama'gite mne, pa'ʒaləstə]
I've got a problem.	**У меня проблема.** [u me'ɲa prab'lema]
I don't feel well.	**Мне плохо.** [mne 'plɔhə]
Call an ambulance!	**Вызовите скорую!** [vɪzawite 'skorʊʲʉ!]
May I make a call?	**Могу я позвонить?** [ma'gʊ ja pazva'nitʲ?]

I'm sorry.	**Извините.** [izwi'nite]
You're welcome.	**Пожалуйста.** [pa'ʒaləstə]

I, me	**я** [ja]
you (inform.)	**ты** [tɪ]
he	**он** [ɔn]
she	**она** [a'na]
they (masc.)	**они** [a'ni]
they (fem.)	**они** [a'ni]
we	**мы** [mɪ]
you (pl)	**вы** [vɪ]
you (sg, form.)	**Вы** [vɪ]

ENTRANCE	**ВХОД** [vhɔt]
EXIT	**ВЫХОД** ['vɪhət]
OUT OF ORDER	**НЕ РАБОТАЕТ** [ne ra'bɔtaet]
CLOSED	**ЗАКРЫТО** [zak'rɪtə]

OPEN

FOR WOMEN

FOR MEN

ОТКРЫТО
[atk'rɪtə]

ДЛЯ ЖЕНЩИН
[dʎa 'ʒɛnɕin]

ДЛЯ МУЖЧИН
[dʎa mʊ'ɕin]

T&P BOOKS

CONCISE DICTIONARY

This section contains more
than 1,500 useful words
arranged alphabetically.
The dictionary includes a lot
of gastronomic terms and
will be helpful when ordering
food at a restaurant or buying
groceries

T&P Books Publishing

DICTIONARY CONTENTS

T&P Books Publishing

T&P Books Publishing

time	время (с)	[v'rem'a]
hour	час (м)	[tʃas]
half an hour	полчаса (мн)	[paltʃe'sa]
minute	минута (ж)	[mi'nʊtə]
second	секунда (ж)	[si'kʊndə]
today (adv)	сегодня	[si'vɔdɲa]
tomorrow (adv)	завтра	['zaftrə]
yesterday (adv)	вчера	[ftʃi'ra]
Monday	понедельник (м)	[pani'deʌnik]
Tuesday	вторник (м)	[f'tɔrnik]
Wednesday	среда (ж)	[sre'da]
Thursday	четверг (м)	[tʃit'werk]
Friday	пятница (ж)	['p'atnitsə]
Saturday	суббота (ж)	[sʊ'bɔtə]
Sunday	воскресенье (с)	[vaskri'seɲe]
day	день (м)	[deɲ]
working day	рабочий день (м)	[ra'bɔtʃij deɲ]
public holiday	празник (м)	[p'raznik]
weekend	выходные (мн)	[vɪhad'nɪe]
week	неделя (ж)	[ni'deʌa]
last week (adv)	на прошлой неделе	[na p'rɔʃlaj ni'dele]
next week (adv)	на следующей неделе	[na sle'dʊɕej ni'dele]
sunrise	восход (м) солнца	[vas'hɔt 'sɔntsə]
sunset	закат (м)	[za'kat]
in the morning	утром	['utram]
in the afternoon	после обеда	['pɔsle a'bedə]
in the evening	вечером	['wetʃeram]
tonight (this evening)	сегодня вечером	[si'vɔdɲa 'wetʃeram]
at night	ночью	['nɔtʃjy]
midnight	полночь (ж)	['pɔlnatʃ]
January	январь (м)	[en'var']
February	февраль (м)	[fiv'raʌ]
March	март (м)	[mart]
April	апрель (м)	[ap'reʌ]
May	май (м)	[maj]
June	июнь (м)	[i'juɲ]

July	июль (м)	[i'juʌ]
August	август (м)	['ɑvgʊst]
September	сентябрь (м)	[sin'tʲabrʲ]
October	октябрь (м)	[ɑk'tʲabrʲ]
November	ноябрь (м)	[nɑ'jabrʲ]
December	декабрь (м)	[di'kɑbrʲ]

in spring	весной	[wis'nɔj]
in summer	летом	['letɑm]
in fall	осенью	['ɔseɲy]
in winter	зимой	[zi'mɔj]

month	месяц (м)	['mesiʦ]
season (summer, etc.)	сезон (м)	[si'zɔn]
year	год (м)	[gɔt]
century	век (м)	[wek]

2. Numbers. Numerals

digit, figure	цифра (ж)	['ʦɪfrə]
number	число (с)	[ʧis'lɔ]
minus sign	минус (м)	['minʊs]
plus sign	плюс (м)	[plys]
sum, total	сумма (ж)	['sʊmmə]

first (adj)	первый	['pervɪj]
second (adj)	второй	[ftɑ'rɔj]
third (adj)	третий	[t'retij]

0 zero	ноль	[nɔʌ]
1 one	один	[ɑ'din]
2 two	два	[dvə]
3 three	три	[tri]
4 four	четыре	[ʧɪ'tɪre]

5 five	пять	[pʲatʲ]
6 six	шесть	[ʃəstʲ]
7 seven	семь	[semʲ]
8 eight	восемь	['vɔsemʲ]
9 nine	девять	['dewitʲ]
10 ten	десять	['desitʲ]

11 eleven	одиннадцать	[ɑ'dinɑtsatʲ]
12 twelve	двенадцать	[dwi'nɑtsatʲ]
13 thirteen	тринадцать	[tri'nɑtsatʲ]
14 fourteen	четырнадцать	[ʧɪ'tɪrnɑtsatʲ]
15 fifteen	пятнадцать	[pit'nɑtsatʲ]

| 16 sixteen | шестнадцать | [ʃɛs'nɑtsatʲ] |
| 17 seventeen | семнадцать | [sim'nɑtsatʲ] |

| 18 eighteen | восемнадцать | [vasem'natsatʲ] |
| 19 nineteen | девятнадцать | [diwit'natsatʲ] |

20 twenty	двадцать	[d'vatsatʲ]
30 thirty	тридцать	[t'ritsatʲ]
40 forty	сорок	['sɔrak]
50 fifty	пятьдесят	[pitʲdi'sʲat]

60 sixty	шестьдесят	[ʃistʲdi'sʲat]
70 seventy	семьдесят	['semʲdisit]
80 eighty	восемьдесят	['vɔsemʲdisit]
90 ninety	девяносто	[diwi'nɔstə]

100 one hundred	сто	[stɔ]
200 two hundred	двести	[d'westi]
300 three hundred	триста	[t'ristə]
400 four hundred	четыреста	[tʃi'tɪrestə]
500 five hundred	пятьсот	[pi'tsɔt]

600 six hundred	шестьсот	[ʃɛs'sɔt]
700 seven hundred	семьсот	[simʲ'sɔt]
800 eight hundred	восемьсот	[vasemʲ'sɔt]
900 nine hundred	девятьсот	[diwi'tsɔt]
1000 one thousand	тысяча	['tɪsitʃə]

| 10000 ten thousand | десять тысяч | ['desitʲ 'tɪsitʃ] |
| one hundred thousand | сто тысяч | [stɔ 'tɪsitʃ] |

| million | миллион (м) | [mili'ɔn] |
| billion | миллиард (м) | [mili'art] |

3. Humans. Family

man (adult male)	мужчина (м)	[mʊ'ɕinə]
young man	юноша (м)	['junaʃe]
teenager	подросток (м)	[pad'rɔstak]
woman	женщина (ж)	['ʒɛɲɕinə]
girl (young woman)	девушка (ж)	['devʊʃkə]

age	возраст (м)	['vɔzrast]
adult (adj)	взрослый	[vz'rɔslɪj]
middle-aged (adj)	средних лет	[s'rednih let]
elderly (adj)	пожилой	[paʒɪ'lɔj]
old (adj)	старый	[s'tarɪj]

old man	старик (м)	[sta'rik]
old woman	старая женщина (м)	[s'taraja 'ʒɛɲɕinə]
retirement	пенсия (ж)	['peɲsija]
to retire (from job)	уйти на пенсию	[uj'ti na 'peɲsiju]
retiree	пенсионер (ж)	[piɲsia'ner]

mother	мать (ж)	[matʲ]
father	отец (м)	[a'tets]
son	сын (м)	[sɪn]
daughter	дочь (ж)	[dotʃ]
brother	брат (м)	[brat]
sister	сестра (ж)	[sist'ra]

parents	родители (мн)	[ra'diteli]
child	ребёнок (м)	[ri'bɜnak]
children	дети (мн)	['deti]
stepmother	мачеха (ж)	['matʃehə]
stepfather	отчим (м)	['otʃim]

grandmother	бабушка (ж)	['babuʃkə]
grandfather	дедушка (м)	['deduʃkə]
grandson	внук (м)	[vnʊk]
granddaughter	внучка (ж)	[v'nutʃkə]
grandchildren	внуки (мн)	[v'nʊki]

uncle	дядя (м)	['dʲadʲa]
aunt	тётя (ж)	['tɜtʲa]
nephew	племянник (м)	[pli'mʲanik]
niece	племянница (ж)	[pli'mʲanitsə]

wife	жена (ж)	[ʒɪ'na]
husband	муж (м)	[mʊʃ]
married (masc.)	женатый	[ʒɪ'natij]
married (fem.)	замужняя	[za'mʊʒnija]
widow	вдова (ж)	[vda'va]
widower	вдовец (м)	[vda'wets]

| name (first name) | имя (с) | ['imʲa] |
| surname (last name) | фамилия (ж) | [fa'milija] |

relative	родственник (м)	['rotstwenik]
friend (masc.)	друг (м)	[drʊk]
friendship	дружба (ж)	[d'rʊʒbə]

partner	партнёр (м)	[part'nɜr]
superior (n)	начальник (м)	[na'tʃaʎnik]
colleague	коллега (м)	[ka'legə]
neighbors	соседи (мн)	[sa'sedi]

4. Human body

organism (body)	организм (м)	[arga'nizm]
body	тело (с)	['telə]
heart	сердце (с)	['sertsе]
blood	кровь (ж)	[krofʲ]
brain	мозг (м)	[mɔsk]

nerve	нерв (м)	[nerf]
bone	кость (ж)	[kostʲ]
skeleton	скелет (м)	[ski'let]
spine (backbone)	позвоночник (м)	[pazva'notʃnik]
rib	ребро (с)	[rib'rɔ]
skull	череп (м)	['tʃerep]

muscle	мышца (ж)	['mɪʃtsə]
lungs	лёгкие (мн)	['lɔɦkie]
skin	кожа (ж)	['kɔʒə]

head	голова (ж)	[gala'va]
face	лицо (с)	[li'tsɔ]
nose	нос (м)	[nɔs]
forehead	лоб (м)	[lɔp]
cheek	щека (ж)	[ɕi'ka]

mouth	рот (м)	[rɔt]
tongue	язык (м)	[ja'zɪk]
tooth	зуб (м)	[zup]
lips	губы (мн)	['gʊbɪ]
chin	подбородок (м)	[padba'rɔdak]

ear	ухо (с)	['uhə]
neck	шея (ж)	[ʃəja]
throat	горло (с)	['gɔrlə]

eye	глаз (м)	[glas]
pupil	зрачок (м)	[zra'tʃɔk]
eyebrow	бровь (ж)	[brɔfʲ]
eyelash	ресница (ж)	[ris'nitsə]

hair	волосы (мн)	['vɔlasɪ]
hairstyle	причёска (ж)	[pri'tʃɔskə]
mustache	усы (м мн)	[u'sɪ]
beard	борода (ж)	[bara'da]
to have (a beard, etc.)	носить	[na'sitʲ]
bald (adj)	лысый	['lɪsɪj]

hand	кисть (ж)	[kistʲ]
arm	рука (ж)	[rʊ'ka]
finger	палец (м)	['palets]
nail	ноготь (м)	['nɔgatʲ]
palm	ладонь (ж)	[la'dɔɲ]

shoulder	плечо (с)	[pli'tʃɔ]
leg	нога (ж)	[na'ga]
foot	ступня (ж)	[stʊp'ɲa]
knee	колено (с)	[ka'lenə]
heel	пятка (ж)	['pʲatkə]
back	спина (ж)	[spi'na]
waist	талия (ж)	['talija]

beauty mark	родинка (ж)	['rɔdinkə]
birthmark	родимое пятно (с)	[ra'dimae pit'nɔ]
(café au lait spot)		

5. Medicine. Diseases. Drugs

health	здоровье (с)	[zda'rɔvje]
well (not sick)	здоровый	[zda'rɔvɪj]
sickness	болезнь (ж)	[ba'lezn]
to be sick	болеть	[ba'letʲ]
ill, sick (adj)	больной	[baʎ'nɔj]

cold (illness)	простуда (ж)	[pras'tʊdə]
to catch a cold	простудиться	[prastʊ'ditsə]
tonsillitis	ангина (ж)	[a'ŋinə]
pneumonia	воспаление (с) лёгких	[vaspa'lenie 'lʒɦkih]
flu, influenza	грипп (м)	[grip]

runny nose (coryza)	насморк (м)	['nasmark]
cough	кашель (м)	['kaʃəʎ]
to cough (vi)	кашлять	['kaʃlitʲ]
to sneeze (vi)	чихать	[ʧi'hatʲ]

stroke	инсульт (м)	[in'sʊʎt]
heart attack	инфаркт (м)	[in'farkt]
allergy	аллергия (ж)	[alir'gija]
asthma	астма (ж)	['astmə]
diabetes	диабет (м)	[dia'bet]

tumor	опухоль (ж)	['ɔpʊhaʎ]
cancer	рак (м)	[rak]
alcoholism	алкоголизм (м)	[alkaga'lizm]
AIDS	СПИД (м)	[spit]
fever	лихорадка (ж)	[liha'ratkə]
seasickness	морская болезнь (ж)	[mars'kaja ba'lezn]

bruise (hématome)	синяк (м)	[si'ɲak]
bump (lump)	шишка (ж)	['ʃiʃkə]
to limp (vi)	хромать	[hra'matʲ]
dislocation	вывих (м)	['vɪwih]
to dislocate (vt)	вывихнуть	['vɪwihnʊtʲ]

fracture	перелом (м)	[pere'lɔm]
burn (injury)	ожог (м)	[a'ʒɔk]
injury	повреждение (с)	[pavreʒ'denie]
pain	боль (ж)	[bɔʎ]
toothache	зубная боль (ж)	[zub'naja bɔʎ]

| to sweat (perspire) | потеть | [pa'tetʲ] |
| deaf (adj) | глухой | [glu'hɔj] |

mute (adj)	немой	[ni'mɔj]
immunity	иммунитет (м)	[imʊni'tet]
virus	вирус (м)	['wirʊs]
microbe	микроб (м)	[mik'rɔp]
bacterium	бактерия (ж)	[bak'tɛrija]
infection	инфекция (ж)	[in'fektsɪja]

hospital	больница (ж)	[baʎ'nitsə]
cure	лечение (с)	[li'ʧenie]
to vaccinate (vt)	делать прививку	['delatʲ pri'wifkʊ]
to be in a coma	быть в коме	[bɪtʲ f 'kɔme]
intensive care	реанимация (ж)	[riani'matsɪja]
symptom	симптом (м)	[simp'tɔm]
pulse	пульс (м)	[pʊʎs]

6. Feelings. Emotions. Conversation

I, me	я	[ja]
you	ты	[tɪ]
he	он	[ɔn]
she	она	[a'na]
it	оно	[a'nɔ]

we	мы	[mɪ]
you (to a group)	вы	[vɪ]
they	они	[a'ni]

Hello! (fam.)	Здравствуй!	[zd'rastvʊj]
Hello! (form.)	Здравствуйте!	[zd'rastvʊjte]
Good morning!	Доброе утро!	['dɔbrae 'utra]
Good afternoon!	Добрый день!	['dɔbrɪj deɲ]
Good evening!	Добрый вечер!	['dɔbrɪj 'weʧer]

to say hello	здороваться	[zda'rɔvatsə]
to greet (vt)	приветствовать	[pri'wetstvavatʲ]
How are you? (form.)	Как у вас дела?	[kak u vas di'la]
How are you? (fam.)	Как дела?	[kak di'la]
Bye-Bye! Goodbye!	До свидания!	[da swi'danija]
Thank you!	Спасибо!	[spa'siba]

feelings	чувства (с мн)	['ʧustvə]
to be hungry	хотеть есть	[ha'tetʲ 'estʲ]
to be thirsty	хотеть пить	[ha'tetʲ 'pitʲ]
tired (adj)	усталый	[us'talɪj]

to be worried	беспокоиться	[bispa'kɔitsə]
to be nervous	нервничать	['nervniʧatʲ]
hope	надежда (ж)	[na'deʒdə]
to hope (vi, vt)	надеяться	[na'deitsə]
character	характер (м)	[ha'rakter]

modest (adj)	скромный	[sk'rɔmnɪj]
lazy (adj)	ленивый	[li'nivɪj]
generous (adj)	щедрый	['ɕedrɪj]
talented (adj)	талантливый	[ta'lantlivɪj]
honest (adj)	честный	['tʃesnɪj]
serious (adj)	серьёзный	[si'rjoznɪj]
shy, timid (adj)	робкий	['rɔpkij]
sincere (adj)	искренний	['iskrenij]
coward	трус (м)	[trʊs]
to sleep (vi)	спать	[spatʲ]
dream	сон (м)	[sɔn]
bed	кровать (ж)	[kra'vatʲ]
pillow	подушка (ж)	[pa'dʊʃkə]
insomnia	бессонница (ж)	[bi'sɔnitsə]
to go to bed	идти спать	[itʲti s'patʲ]
nightmare	кошмар (м)	[kaʃ'mar]
alarm clock	будильник (м)	[bʊ'diʎnik]
smile	улыбка (ж)	[u'lɪpkə]
to smile (vi)	улыбаться	[ulɪ'batsə]
to laugh (vi)	смеяться	[smi'jatsə]
quarrel	ссора (ж)	[s'sɔrə]
insult	оскорбление (с)	[askarb'lenie]
resentment	обида (ж)	[a'bidə]
angry (mad)	сердитый	[sir'ditɪj]

7. Clothing. Personal accessories

clothes	одежда (ж)	[a'deʒdə]
coat (overcoat)	пальто (с)	[paʎ'tɔ]
fur coat	шуба (ж)	['ʃubə]
jacket (e.g., leather ~)	куртка (ж)	['kʊrtkə]
raincoat (trenchcoat, etc.)	плащ (м)	[plaɕ]
shirt (button shirt)	рубашка (ж)	[rʊ'baʃkə]
pants	брюки (мн)	[b'ryki]
suit jacket	пиджак (м)	[pi'dʒak]
suit	костюм (м)	[kas'tym]
dress (frock)	платье (с)	[p'latje]
skirt	юбка (ж)	['jupkə]
T-shirt	футболка (ж)	[fʊd'bɔlkə]
bathrobe	халат (м)	[ha'lat]
pajamas	пижама (ж)	[pi'ʒamə]
workwear	рабочая одежда (ж)	[ra'botʃija a'deʒdə]
underwear	бельё (с)	[bi'ʎjo]

socks	носки (мн)	[nas'ki]
bra	бюстгальтер (м)	[bys'gaʌtɛr]
pantyhose	колготки (мн)	[kal'gotki]
stockings (thigh highs)	чулки (мн)	[ʧul'ki]
bathing suit	купальник (м)	[kʊ'paʌnik]

hat	шапка (ж)	['ʃʌpkə]
footwear	обувь (ж)	['ɔbʊfʲ]
boots (cowboy ~)	сапоги (мн)	[sapa'gi]
heel	каблук (м)	[kab'luk]
shoestring	шнурок (м)	[ʃnʊ'rɔk]
shoe polish	крем (м) для обуви	[krem dʌa 'ɔbʊwi]

cotton (n)	хлопок (м)	[h'lɔpak]
wool (n)	шерсть (ж)	[ʃɛrstʲ]
fur (n)	мех (м)	[meh]

gloves	перчатки (ж мн)	[pir'ʧatki]
mittens	варежки (ж мн)	['variʃki]
scarf (muffler)	шарф (м)	[ʃʌrf]
glasses (eyeglasses)	очки (мн)	[aʧ'ki]
umbrella	зонт (м)	[zɔnt]

tie (necktie)	галстук (м)	['galstʊk]
handkerchief	носовой платок (м)	[nasa'vɔj pla'tɔk]
comb	расчёска (ж)	[ra'ɕɜskə]
hairbrush	щётка (ж) для волос	['ɕɜtka dʌa va'lɔs]

buckle	пряжка (ж)	[p'rʲaʃkə]
belt	пояс (м)	['pɔis]
purse	сумочка (ж)	['sʊmaʧkə]

collar	воротник (м)	[varat'nik]
pocket	карман (м)	[kar'man]
sleeve	рукав (м)	[rʊ'kaf]
fly (on trousers)	ширинка (ж)	[ʃi'rinkə]

zipper (fastener)	молния (ж)	['mɔlnija]
button	пуговица (ж)	['pʊgawitsə]
to get dirty (vi)	испачкаться	[is'paʧkatsə]
stain (mark, spot)	пятно (с)	[pit'nɔ]

8. City. Urban institutions

store	магазин (м)	[maga'zin]
shopping mall	торговый центр (м)	[tar'gɔvij tsɛntr]
supermarket	супермаркет (м)	[sʊper'market]
shoe store	обувной магазин (м)	[abʊv'nɔj maga'zin]
bookstore	книжный магазин (м)	[k'niʒnij maga'zin]
drugstore, pharmacy	аптека (ж)	[ap'tekə]

bakery	булочная (ж)	['bʊlatʃnaja]
candy store	кондитерская (ж)	[kan'diterskaja]
grocery store	бакалея (ж)	[baka'leja]
butcher shop	мясная лавка (ж)	[mʲas'naja 'lafkə]
produce store	овощная лавка (ж)	[avaɕ'naja 'lafkə]
market	рынок (м)	['rɪnak]

hair salon	парикмахерская (ж)	[parih'maherskaja]
post office	почта (ж)	['potʃtə]
dry cleaners	химчистка (ж)	[him'tʃistkə]
circus	цирк (м)	[tsɪrk]
zoo	зоопарк (м)	[zaa'park]

theater	театр (м)	[ti'atr]
movie theater	кинотеатр (м)	[kinati'atr]
museum	музей (м)	[mʊ'zej]
library	библиотека (ж)	[biblia'tekə]

mosque	мечеть (ж)	[mi'tʃetʲ]
synagogue	синагога (ж)	[sina'gɔgə]
cathedral	собор (м)	[sa'bɔr]
temple	храм (м)	[hram]
church	церковь (ж)	['tsərkafʲ]

college	институт (м)	[insti'tʊt]
university	университет (м)	[uniwersi'tet]
school	школа (ж)	[ʃ'kɔlə]
hotel	гостиница (ж)	[gas'tinitsə]
bank	банк (м)	[bank]
embassy	посольство (с)	[pa'soʎstvə]
travel agency	турагентство (с)	[tʊra'genstvə]

subway	метро (с)	[mit'rɔ]
hospital	больница (ж)	[baʎ'nitsə]
gas station	бензозаправка (ж)	[binzazap'rafkə]
parking lot	стоянка (ж)	[sta'jankə]

ENTRANCE	ВХОД	[vhɔt]
EXIT	ВЫХОД	['vɪhat]
PUSH	ОТ СЕБЯ	[at se'bʲa]
PULL	НА СЕБЯ	[na se'bʲa]
OPEN	ОТКРЫТО	[atk'rɪtə]
CLOSED	ЗАКРЫТО	[zak'rɪtə]

monument	памятник (м)	['pamitnik]
fortress	крепость (ж)	[k'repastʲ]
palace	дворец (м)	[dva'rets]

medieval (adj)	средневековый	[sredniwi'kɔvɪj]
ancient (adj)	старинный	[sta'rinnɪj]
national (adj)	национальный	[natsɪa'naʎnɪj]
well-known (adj)	известный	[iz'wesnɪj]

9. Money. Finances

money	деньги (мн)	['deŋgi]
coin	монета (ж)	[ma'netə]
dollar	доллар (м)	['dɔllar]
euro	евро (с)	['evrə]
ATM	банкомат (м)	[banka'mat]
currency exchange	обменный пункт (м)	[ab'mennɪj punkt]
exchange rate	курс (м)	[kurs]
cash	наличные деньги (мн)	[na'liʧnɪe 'deŋgi]
How much?	Сколько?	[s'kɔʎka]
to pay (vi, vt)	платить	[pla'titʲ]
payment	оплата (ж)	[ap'latə]
change (give the ~)	сдача (ж)	[z'daʧə]
price	цена (ж)	[tsɪ'na]
discount	скидка (ж)	[s'kitkə]
cheap (adj)	дешёвый	[di'ʃovɪj]
expensive (adj)	дорогой	[dara'gɔj]
bank	банк (м)	[bank]
account	счёт (м)	['ɕɜt]
credit card	кредитная карта (ж)	[kri'ditnaja 'kartə]
check	чек (м)	[ʧek]
to write a check	выписать чек	['vɪpisatʲ ʧek]
checkbook	чековая книжка (ж)	['ʧekavaja k'niʃkə]
debt	долг (м)	[dɔlk]
debtor	должник (м)	[daʒ'nik]
to lend (money)	дать в долг	[datʲ v 'dɔlk]
to borrow (vi, vt)	взять в долг	[vzʲatʲ v 'dɔlk]
to rent (~ a tuxedo)	взять напрокат	[vzʲatʲ napra'kat]
on credit (adv)	в кредит	[f kre'dit]
wallet	бумажник (м)	[bu'maʒnik]
safe	сейф (м)	[sɛjf]
inheritance	наследство (с)	[nas'letstvə]
fortune (wealth)	состояние (с)	[sasta'janie]
tax	налог (м)	[na'lɔk]
fine	штраф (м)	[ʃtraf]
to fine (vt)	штрафовать	[ʃtrafa'vatʲ]
wholesale (adj)	оптовый	[ap'tɔvɪj]
retail (adj)	розничный	['rɔzniʧnɪj]
to insure (vt)	страховать	[straha'vatʲ]
insurance	страховка (ж)	[stra'hɔfkə]
capital	капитал (м)	[kapi'tal]
turnover	оборот (м)	[aba'rɔt]

stock (share)	акция (ж)	['aktsɪja]
profit	прибыль (ж)	[p'ribɪʎ]
profitable (adj)	прибыльный	[p'ribɪʎnɪj]

crisis	кризис (м)	[k'rizis]
bankruptcy	банкротство (с)	[bank'rɔtstvə]
to go bankrupt	обанкротиться	[abank'rɔtitsə]

accountant	бухгалтер (м)	[bʊ'galter]
salary	заработная плата (ж)	['zarabatnaja p'latə]
bonus (money)	премия (ж)	[p'remija]

10. Transportation

bus	автобус (м)	[af'tɔbʊs]
streetcar	трамвай (м)	[tram'vaj]
trolley bus	троллейбус (м)	[tra'lejbʊs]

to go by ...	ехать на ...	['ehatⁱ na]
to get on (~ the bus)	сесть на ...	[sestⁱ na]
to get off ...	сойти с ...	[saj'ti s]

stop (e.g., bus ~)	остановка (ж)	[asta'nɔfkə]
terminus	конечная остановка (ж)	[ka'netʃnaja asta'nɔfkə]
schedule	расписание (с)	[raspi'sanie]
ticket	билет (м)	[bi'let]
to be late (for ...)	опаздывать на ...	[a'pazdɪvatⁱ na]

taxi, cab	такси (с)	[tak'si]
by taxi	на такси	[na tak'si]
taxi stand	стоянка (ж) такси	[sta'janka tak'si]

traffic	уличное движение (с)	['ulitʃnae dwi'ʒɛnie]
rush hour	часы пик (м)	[tʃə'sɪ pik]
to park (vi)	парковаться	[parka'vatsə]

subway	метро (с)	[mit'rɔ]
station	станция (ж)	[s'tantsɪja]
train	поезд (м)	['pɔezt]
train station	вокзал (м)	[vak'zal]
rails	рельсы (мн)	['reʎsɪ]
compartment	купе (с)	[kʊ'pɛ]
berth	полка (ж)	['pɔlkə]

airplane	самолёт (м)	[sama'lɜt]
air ticket	авиабилет (м)	[awiabi'let]
airline	авиакомпания (ж)	[awiakam'panija]
airport	аэропорт (м)	[aəra'pɔrt]
flight (act of flying)	полёт (м)	[pa'lɜt]
luggage	багаж (м)	[ba'gaʃ]

luggage cart	тележка (ж) для багажа	[ti'leʃka dʌa baga'ʒa]
ship	корабль (м)	[ka'rabʌ]
cruise ship	лайнер (м)	['lajner]
yacht	яхта (ж)	['jahtə]
boat (flat-bottomed ~)	лодка (ж)	['lɔtkə]

captain	капитан (м)	[kapi'tan]
cabin	каюта (ж)	[ka'jutə]
port (harbor)	порт (м)	[pɔrt]

bicycle	велосипед (м)	[wilasi'pet]
scooter	мотороллер (м)	[mata'rɔler]
motorcycle, bike	мотоцикл (м)	[mata'tsɪkl]
pedal	педаль (ж)	[pi'daʌ]
pump	насос (м)	[na'sɔs]
wheel	колесо (с)	[kale'sɔ]

automobile, car	автомобиль (м)	[aftama'biʌ]
ambulance	скорая помощь (ж)	[s'kɔraja 'pɔmaɕ]
truck	грузовик (м)	[gruzа'wik]
used (adj)	подержанный	[pa'derʒenɪj]
car crash	авария (ж)	[a'varija]
repair	ремонт (м)	[ri'mɔnt]

11. Food. Part 1

meat	мясо (с)	['mʲasə]
chicken	курица (ж)	['kuritsə]
duck	утка (ж)	['utkə]

pork	свинина (ж)	[swi'ninə]
veal	телятина (ж)	[ti'ʌatinə]
lamb	баранина (ж)	[ba'raninə]
beef	говядина (ж)	[ga'vʲadinə]

sausage (bologna, pepperoni, etc.)	колбаса (ж)	[kalba'sa]
egg	яйцо (с)	[jaj'tsɔ]
fish	рыба (ж)	['rɪbə]
cheese	сыр (м)	[sɪr]
sugar	сахар (м)	['sahar]
salt	соль (ж)	[sɔʌ]

rice	рис (м)	[ris]
pasta	макароны (мн)	[maka'rɔnɪ]
butter	сливочное масло (с)	[s'livatʃnae 'maslə]
vegetable oil	растительное масло (с)	[ras'titeʌnae 'maslə]
bread	хлеб (м)	[hlep]
chocolate (n)	шоколад (м)	[ʃʌka'lat]
wine	вино (с)	[wi'nɔ]

coffee	кофе (м)	['kɔfe]
milk	молоко (с)	[mala'kɔ]
juice	сок (м)	[sɔk]
beer	пиво (с)	['pive]
tea	чай (м)	[tʃaj]

tomato	помидор (м)	[pami'dɔr]
cucumber	огурец (м)	[agʊ'rets]
carrot	морковь (ж)	[mar'kɔfʲ]
potato	картофель (м)	[kar'tɔfeʎ]
onion	лук (м)	[luk]
garlic	чеснок (м)	[tʃis'nɔk]

cabbage	капуста (ж)	[ka'pʊstə]
beetroot	свёкла (ж)	['swɜklə]
eggplant	баклажан (м)	[bakla'ʒan]
dill	укроп (м)	[uk'rɔp]
lettuce	салат (м)	[sa'lat]
corn (maize)	кукуруза (ж)	[kʊkʊ'rʊzə]

fruit	фрукт (м)	[frʊkt]
apple	яблоко (с)	['jablakə]
pear	груша (ж)	[g'rʊʃə]
lemon	лимон (м)	[li'mɔn]
orange	апельсин (м)	[apiʎ'sin]
strawberry	клубника (ж)	[klub'nikə]

plum	слива (ж)	[s'livə]
raspberry	малина (ж)	[ma'linə]
pineapple	ананас (м)	[ana'nas]
banana	банан (м)	[ba'nan]
watermelon	арбуз (м)	[ar'bʊs]
grape	виноград (м)	[winag'rat]
melon	дыня (ж)	['dɪɲa]

12. Food. Part 2

cuisine	кухня (ж)	['kʊhɲa]
recipe	рецепт (м)	[ri'tsəpt]
food	еда (ж)	[e'da]

to have breakfast	завтракать	['zaftrakatʲ]
to have lunch	обедать	[a'bedatʲ]
to have dinner	ужинать	['ʊʒɪnatʲ]

taste, flavor	вкус (м)	[fkʊs]
tasty (adj)	вкусный	[f'kʊsnɪj]
cold (adj)	холодный	[ha'lɔdnɪj]
hot (adj)	горячий	[ga'rʲatʃij]
sweet (sugary)	сладкий	[s'latkij]

salty (adj)	солёный	[sɑ'lɛnɪj]
sandwich (bread)	бутерброд (м)	[buterb'rɔt]
side dish	гарнир (м)	[gɑr'nir]
filling (for cake, pie)	начинка (ж)	[nɑ'ʧinkə]
sauce	соус (м)	['sɔus]
piece (of cake, pie)	кусок (м)	[ku'sɔk]

diet	диета (ж)	[di'etə]
vitamin	витамин (м)	[witɑ'min]
calorie	калория (ж)	[kɑ'lɔrija]
vegetarian (n)	вегетарианец (м)	[wigitɑri'ɑnets]

restaurant	ресторан (м)	[ristɑ'rɑn]
coffee house	кофейня (ж)	[kɑ'fejnɑ]
appetite	аппетит (м)	[ɑpi'tit]
Enjoy your meal!	Приятного аппетита!	[pri'jatnɑvɑ ɑpe'tita]

waiter	официант (м)	[ɑfitsı'ɑnt]
waitress	официантка (ж)	[ɑfitsı'ɑntkə]
bartender	бармен (м)	[bɑr'men]
menu	меню (с)	[mi'ny]

spoon	ложка (ж)	['lɔʃkə]
knife	нож (м)	[nɔʃ]
fork	вилка (ж)	['wilkə]
cup (e.g., coffee ~)	чашка (ж)	['ʧaʃkə]
plate (dinner ~)	тарелка (ж)	[tɑ'relkə]
saucer	блюдце (с)	[b'lytse]
napkin (on table)	салфетка (ж)	[sɑl'fetkə]
toothpick	зубочистка (ж)	[zubɑ'ʧistkə]

to order (meal)	заказать	[zɑkɑ'zatⁱ]
course, dish	блюдо (с)	[b'lydə]
portion	порция (ж)	['pɔrtsija]
appetizer	закуска (ж)	[zɑ'kuskə]
salad	салат (м)	[sɑ'lɑt]
soup	суп (м)	[sup]

dessert	десерт (м)	[di'sert]
whole fruit jam	варенье (с)	[vɑ'renje]
ice-cream	мороженое (с)	[mɑ'rɔʒnɑe]

check	счёт (м)	['ɕɛt]
to pay the check	оплатить счёт	[ɑplɑ'titⁱ 'ɕɛt]
tip	чаевые (мн)	[ʧⁱi'vɪe]

13. House. Apartment. Part 1

| house | дом (м) | [dɔm] |
| country house | загородный дом (м) | ['zagɑrɑdnɪj dɔm] |

villa (seaside ~)	вилла (ж)	['willə]
floor, story	этаж (м)	[ɛ'taʃ]
entrance	подъезд (м)	[padʰ'ezt]
wall	стена (ж)	[sti'na]
roof	крыша (ж)	[k'rɪʃə]
chimney	труба (ж)	[trʊ'ba]
attic (storage place)	чердак (м)	[tʃir'dak]

window	окно (с)	[ak'nɔ]
window ledge	подоконник (м)	[pada'kɔnnik]
balcony	балкон (м)	[bal'kɔn]

stairs (stairway)	лестница (ж)	['lesnitsə]
mailbox	почтовый ящик (м)	[patʃ'tovɪj 'jaɕik]
garbage can	мусорный бак (м)	['mʊsarnɪj bak]
elevator	лифт (м)	[lift]

electricity	электричество (с)	[ɛlekt'ritʃestvə]
light bulb	лампочка (ж)	['lampatʃkə]
switch	выключатель (м)	[vɪkly'tʃateʌ]
wall socket	розетка (ж)	[ra'zetkə]
fuse	предохранитель (м)	[pridahra'niteʌ]

door	дверь (ж)	[dwerʲ]
handle, doorknob	ручка (ж)	['rʊtʃkə]
key	ключ (м)	[klytʃ]
doormat	коврик (м)	['kɔvrik]

door lock	замок (м)	[za'mɔk]
doorbell	звонок (м)	[zva'nɔk]
knock (at the door)	стук (м)	[stʊk]
to knock (vi)	стучать	[stʊ'tʃatʲ]
peephole	глазок (м)	[gla'zɔk]

yard	двор (м)	[dvɔr]
garden	сад (м)	[sat]
swimming pool	бассейн (м)	[ba'sɛjn]
gym (home gym)	тренажёрный зал (м)	[trina'ʒɔrnɪj zal]
tennis court	теннисный корт (м)	['tɛnisnɪj kɔrt]
garage	гараж (м)	[ga'raʃ]

private property	частная собственность (ж)	['tʃasnaja 'sɔpstwenastʲ]
warning sign	предупреждающая надпись (ж)	[pridʊpriʒ'dajuɕeja 'natpisʲ]
security	охрана (ж)	[ah'ranə]
security guard	охранник (м)	[ah'rannik]

renovations	ремонт (м)	[ri'mɔnt]
to renovate (vt)	делать ремонт	['delatʲ re'mɔnt]
to put in order	приводить в порядок	[priva'ditʲ f pa'rʲadak]
to paint (~ a wall)	красить	[k'rasitʲ]

wallpaper	обои (мн)	[a'bɔi]
to varnish (vt)	покрывать лаком	[pakrı'vatʲ 'lakam]
pipe	труба (ж)	[tru'ba]
tools	инструменты (м мн)	[instru'mentı]
basement	подвал (м)	[pad'val]
sewerage (system)	канализация (ж)	[kanali'zatsıja]

14. House. Apartment. Part 2

apartment	квартира (ж)	[kvar'tirə]
room	комната (ж)	['komnatə]
bedroom	спальня (ж)	[s'paʎna]
dining room	столовая (ж)	[sta'lɔvaja]
living room	гостиная (ж)	[gas'tinaja]
study (home office)	кабинет (м)	[kabi'net]
entry room	прихожая (ж)	[pri'hoʒaja]
bathroom (room with a bath or shower)	ванная комната (ж)	['vannaja 'komnatə]
half bath	туалет (м)	[tua'let]
floor	пол (м)	[pol]
ceiling	потолок (м)	[pata'lɔk]
to dust (vt)	вытирать пыль	[vıti'ratʲ pıʎ]
vacuum cleaner	пылесос (м)	[pıle'sɔs]
to vacuum (vt)	пылесосить	[pıle'sɔsitʲ]
mop	швабра (ж)	[ʃ'vabrə]
dust cloth	тряпка (ж)	[t'rʲapkə]
short broom	веник (м)	['wenik]
dustpan	совок (м) для мусора	[sa'vɔk dʎa 'musarə]
furniture	мебель (ж)	['mebeʎ]
table	стол (м)	[stol]
chair	стул (м)	[stul]
armchair	кресло (с)	[k'reslə]
bookcase	книжный шкаф (м)	[k'niʒnıj ʃkaf]
shelf	полка (ж)	['pɔlkə]
wardrobe	гардероб (м)	[garde'rɔp]
mirror	зеркало (с)	['zerkalə]
carpet	ковёр (м)	[ka'wɜr]
fireplace	камин (м)	[ka'min]
drapes	шторы (ж мн)	[ʃ'tɔrı]
table lamp	настольная лампа (ж)	[nas'tɔʎnaja 'lampə]
chandelier	люстра (ж)	['lystrə]
kitchen	кухня (ж)	['kuhɲa]

gas stove (range)	газовая плита (ж)	['gɑzɑvɑjɑ pli'tɑ]
electric stove	электроплита (ж)	[ɛlektrɑpli'tɑ]
microwave oven	микроволновая печь (ж)	[mikrɑvɑl'nɔvɑjɑ petʃ]
refrigerator	холодильник (м)	[hɑlɑ'diʌnik]
freezer	морозильник (м)	[mɑrɑ'ziʌnik]
dishwasher	посудомоечная машина (ж)	[pɑsʊdɑ'mɔetʃnɑjɑ mɑ'ʃinə]
faucet	кран (м)	[krɑn]
meat grinder	мясорубка (ж)	[misɑ'rʊpkə]
juicer	соковыжималка (ж)	[sɔkɑvɪʒɪ'mɑlkə]
toaster	тостер (м)	['tɔster]
mixer	миксер (м)	['mikser]
coffee machine	кофеварка (ж)	[kɑfe'vɑrkə]
kettle	чайник (м)	['tʃajnik]
teapot	чайник (м)	['tʃajnik]
TV set	телевизор (м)	[tile'wizɑr]
VCR (video recorder)	видеомагнитофон (м)	['wideɑ mɑgnitɑ'fɔn]
iron (e.g., steam ~)	утюг (м)	[u'tyk]
telephone	телефон (м)	[tile'fɔn]

15. Professions. Social status

director	директор (м)	[di'rektɑr]
superior	начальник (м)	[nɑ'tʃaʌnik]
president	президент (м)	[prizi'dent]
assistant	помощник (м)	[pɑ'mɔʃnik]
secretary	секретарь (м)	[sikre'tarʲ]
owner, proprietor	владелец (м)	[vlɑ'delets]
partner	партнёр (м)	[pɑrt'nɜr]
stockholder	акционер (м)	[ɑktsɪɑ'ner]
businessman	бизнесмен (м)	[biznes'men]
millionaire	миллионер (м)	[miliɑ'ner]
billionaire	миллиардер (м)	[miliɑr'der]
actor	актёр (м)	[ɑk'tɜr]
architect	архитектор (м)	[ɑrhi'tektɑr]
banker	банкир (м)	[bɑ'ŋkir]
broker	брокер (м)	[b'rɔker]
veterinarian	ветеринар (м)	[witeri'nɑr]
doctor	врач (м)	[vrɑtʃ]
chambermaid	горничная (ж)	['gɔrnitʃnɑjɑ]
designer	дизайнер (м)	[di'zɑjner]
correspondent	корреспондент (м)	[kɑrespɑn'dent]

delivery man	курьер (м)	[kʊ'rjer]
electrician	электрик (м)	[ɛ'lektrik]
musician	музыкант (м)	[mʊzɪ'kant]
babysitter	няня (ж)	['naɲa]
hairdresser	парикмахер (м)	[parih'maher]
herder, shepherd	пастух (м)	[pas'tʊh]

singer (masc.)	певец (м)	[pi'weʦ]
translator	переводчик (м)	[pire'vɔtʃik]
writer	писатель (м)	[pi'sateʎ]
carpenter	плотник (м)	[p'lɔtnik]
cook	повар (м)	['pɔvar]

fireman	пожарный (м)	[pa'ʒarnɪj]
police officer	полицейский (м)	[pali'ʦejskij]
mailman	почтальон (м)	[paʧta'ʎjon]
programmer	программист (м)	[pragra'mist]
salesman (store staff)	продавец (м)	[prada'weʦ]

worker	рабочий (м)	[ra'bɔʧij]
gardener	садовник (м)	[sa'dɔvnik]
plumber	сантехник (м)	[san'tehnik]
dentist	стоматолог (м)	[stama'tɔlak]
flight attendant (fem.)	стюардесса (ж)	[styar'desə]

dancer (masc.)	танцор (м)	[tan'ʦor]
bodyguard	телохранитель (м)	[tilahra'niteʎ]
scientist	учёный (м)	[u'ʧonɪj]
schoolteacher	учитель (м)	[u'ʧiteʎ]

farmer	фермер (м)	['fermer]
surgeon	хирург (м)	[hi'rʊrk]
miner	шахтёр (м)	[ʃʌh'tɜr]
chef (kitchen chef)	шеф-повар (м)	[ʃɛf'pɔvar]
driver	шофёр (м)	[ʃʌ'fɜr]

16. Sport

kind of sports	вид (м) спорта	[wit s'pɔrtə]
soccer	футбол (м)	[fʊd'bɔl]
hockey	хоккей (м)	[ha'kej]
basketball	баскетбол (м)	[basked'bɔl]
baseball	бейсбол (м)	[bejz'bɔl]

volleyball	волейбол (м)	[valej'bɔl]
boxing	бокс (м)	[bɔks]
wrestling	борьба (ж)	[bar'ba]
tennis	теннис (м)	['tɛnis]
swimming	плавание (с)	[p'lavanie]
chess	шахматы (мн)	['ʃʌhmatɪ]

running	бег (м)	[bek]
athletics	лёгкая атлетика (ж)	['lɔhkaja at'letikə]
figure skating	фигурное катание (с)	[fi'gurnae ka'tanie]
cycling	велоспорт (м)	[wilas'pɔrt]

billiards	бильярд (м)	[bi'ʎjart]
bodybuilding	бодибилдинг (м)	[badi'bildink]
golf	гольф (м)	[gɔʎf]
scuba diving	дайвинг (м)	['dajwink]
sailing	парусный спорт (м)	['parʋsnıj spɔrt]
archery	стрельба (ж) из лука	[streʎ'ba iz 'lukə]

period, half	тайм (м)	[tajm]
half-time	перерыв (м)	[pere'rıf]
tie	ничья (ж)	[ni'ʧja]
to tie (vi)	сыграть вничью	[sıg'ratʲ vni'ʧjy]

treadmill	беговая дорожка (ж)	[biga'vaja da'rɔʃkə]
player	игрок (м)	[ig'rɔk]
substitute	запасной игрок (м)	[zapas'nɔj ig'rɔk]
substitutes bench	скамейка (ж) запасных	[ska'mejka zapas'nıh]
match	матч (м)	[maʧ]
goal	ворота (мн)	[va'rɔtə]
goalkeeper	вратарь (м)	[vra'tarʲ]
goal (score)	гол (м)	[gɔl]

Olympic Games	Олимпийские игры (ж мн)	[alim'pijskie 'igrı]
to set a record	ставить рекорд	[s'tawitʲ re'kɔrt]
final	финал (м)	[fi'nal]
champion	чемпион (м)	[ʧimpi'ɔn]
championship	чемпионат (м)	[ʧimpia'nat]

winner	победитель (м)	[pabi'diteʎ]
victory	победа (ж)	[pa'bedə]
to win (vi)	выиграть	['vıigratʲ]
to lose (not win)	проиграть	[praig'ratʲ]
medal	медаль (ж)	[mi'daʎ]
first place	первое место (с)	['pervae 'mestə]
second place	второе место (с)	[fta'rɔe 'mestə]
third place	третье место (с)	[t'retje 'mestə]

stadium	стадион (м)	[stadi'ɔn]
fan, supporter	болельщик (м)	[ba'leʎɕik]
trainer, coach	тренер (м)	[t'rener]
training	тренировка (ж)	[trini'rɔfkə]

17. Foreign languages. Orthography

| language | язык (м) | [ja'zık] |
| to study (vt) | изучать | [izu'ʧatʲ] |

pronunciation	произношение (c)	[praizna'ʃɛnie]
accent	акцент (м)	[ak'tsənt]
noun	существительное (c)	[suçest'witeʌnae]
adjective	прилагательное (c)	[prila'gateʌnae]
verb	глагол (м)	[gla'gɔl]
adverb	наречие (c)	[na'retʃie]
pronoun	местоимение (c)	[mistai'menie]
interjection	междометие (c)	[meʒda'metie]
preposition	предлог (м)	[prid'lɔk]
root	корень (м) слова	['kɔreɲ s'lɔve]
ending	окончание (c)	[akaɲ'tʃanie]
prefix	приставка (ж)	[pris'tafke]
syllable	слог (м)	[slɔk]
suffix	суффикс (м)	['sufiks]
stress mark	ударение (c)	[uda'renie]
period, dot	точка (ж)	['tɔtʃke]
comma	запятая (ж)	[zapi'taja]
colon	двоеточие (c)	[dvae'tɔtʃie]
ellipsis	многоточие (c)	[mnaga'tɔtʃie]
question	вопрос (м)	[vap'rɔs]
question mark	вопросительный знак (м)	[vapra'siteʌnɪj znak]
exclamation point	восклицательный знак (м)	[vaskli'tsateʌnɪj z'nak]
in quotation marks	в кавычках	[f ka'vɪtʃkah]
in parenthesis	в скобках	[f s'kɔpkah]
letter	буква (ж)	['bukve]
capital letter	большая буква (ж)	[baʌ'ʃʌja 'bukve]
sentence	предложение (c)	[pridla'ʒenie]
group of words	словосочетание (c)	[slɔvasatʃi'tanie]
expression	выражение (c)	[vɪra'ʒɛnie]
subject	подлежащее (c)	[padle'ʒaçee]
predicate	сказуемое (c)	[ska'zuemae]
line	строка (ж)	[stra'ka]
paragraph	абзац (м)	[ab'zats]
synonym	синоним (м)	[si'nɔnim]
antonym	антоним (м)	[an'tɔnim]
exception	исключение (c)	[iskly'tʃenie]
to underline (vt)	подчеркнуть	[patʃerk'nutʲ]
rules	правила (с мн)	[p'rawile]
grammar	грамматика (ж)	[gra'matike]
vocabulary	лексика (ж)	['leksike]

| phonetics | фонетика (ж) | [fɑ'nɛtikə] |
| alphabet | алфавит (м) | [ɑlfɑ'wit] |

textbook	учебник (м)	[u'ʧebnik]
dictionary	словарь (м)	[slɑ'varʲ]
phrasebook	разговорник (м)	[rɑzgɑ'vɔrnik]

word	слово (с)	[s'lɔvə]
meaning	смысл (м)	[smɪsl]
memory	память (ж)	['pɑmitʲ]

18. The Earth. Geography

the Earth	Земля (ж)	[zem'ʎɑ]
the globe (the Earth)	земной шар (м)	[zem'nɔj ʃʌr]
planet	планета (ж)	[plɑ'netə]

geography	география (ж)	[giɑg'rɑfijɑ]
nature	природа (ж)	[pri'rɔdə]
map	карта (ж)	['kɑrtə]
atlas	атлас (м)	['ɑtlɑs]

in the north	на севере	[nɑ 'sewere]
in the south	на юге	[nɑ 'juge]
in the west	на западе	[nɑ 'zɑpɑde]
in the east	на востоке	[nɑ vɑs'tɔke]

sea	море (с)	['mɔre]
ocean	океан (м)	[ɑki'ɑn]
gulf (bay)	залив (м)	[zɑ'lif]
straits	пролив (м)	[prɑ'lif]

continent (mainland)	материк (м)	[mɑte'rik]
island	остров (м)	['ɔstrɑf]
peninsula	полуостров (м)	[pɑlu'ɔstrɑf]
archipelago	архипелаг (м)	[ɑrhipe'lɑk]

harbor	гавань (ж)	['gɑvɑɲ]
coral reef	коралловый риф (м)	[kɑ'rɑlɑvɪj rif]
shore	побережье	[pɑbi'reʒje]
coast	берег (м)	['berek]

| flow (flood tide) | прилив (м) | [pri'lif] |
| ebb (ebb tide) | отлив (м) | [ɑt'lif] |

latitude	широта (ж)	[ʃɪrɑ'tɑ]
longitude	долгота (ж)	[dɑlgɑ'tɑ]
parallel	параллель (ж)	[pɑrɑ'leʎ]
equator	экватор (м)	[ɛk'vɑtɑr]
sky	небо (с)	['nebə]

| horizon | горизонт (м) | [gɑri'zɔnt] |
| atmosphere | атмосфера (ж) | [ɑtmɑs'ferə] |

mountain	гора (ж)	[gɑ'rɑ]
summit, top	вершина (ж)	[wir'ʃinə]
cliff	скала (ж)	[skɑ'lɑ]
hill	холм (м)	[hɔlm]

volcano	вулкан (м)	[vʊl'kɑn]
glacier	ледник (м)	[lid'nik]
waterfall	водопад (м)	[vɑdɑ'pɑt]
plain	равнина (ж)	[rɑv'ninə]

river	река (ж)	[ri'kɑ]
spring (natural source)	источник (м)	[is'tɔtʃnik]
bank (of river)	берег (м)	['berek]
downstream (adv)	вниз по течению	[vnis pɑ ti'tʃeniju]
upstream (adv)	вверх по течению	[werh pɑ ti'tʃeniju]

lake	озеро (c)	['ɔzerə]
dam	плотина (ж)	[plɑ'tinə]
canal	канал (м)	[kɑ'nɑl]
swamp (marshland)	болото (c)	[bɑ'lɔtə]
ice	лёд (м)	['lɔt]

19. Countries of the world. Part 1

Europe	Европа (ж)	[ev'rɔpə]
European Union	Европейский Союз (м)	[evrɑ'pejskij sɑ'jus]
European (n)	европеец (м)	[evrɑ'peets]
European (adj)	европейский	[evrɑ'pejskij]

Austria	Австрия (ж)	['ɑfstrijɑ]
Great Britain	Великобритания (ж)	[wilikɑbri'tɑnijɑ]
England	Англия (ж)	['ɑhglijɑ]
Belgium	Бельгия (ж)	['beʎgijɑ]
Germany	Германия (ж)	[gir'mɑnijɑ]

Netherlands	Нидерланды (мн)	[nider'lɑndɪ]
Holland	Голландия (ж)	[gɑ'lɑndijɑ]
Greece	Греция (ж)	[g'retsijɑ]
Denmark	Дания (ж)	['dɑnijɑ]
Ireland	Ирландия (ж)	[ir'lɑndijɑ]

Iceland	Исландия (ж)	[is'lɑndijɑ]
Spain	Испания (ж)	[is'pɑnijɑ]
Italy	Италия (ж)	[i'tɑlijɑ]
Cyprus	Кипр (м)	[kipr]
Malta	Мальта (ж)	['mɑʎtə]
Norway	Норвегия (ж)	[nɑr'wegijɑ]

Portugal	**Португалия** (ж)	[pɑrtʊ'galija]
Finland	**Финляндия** (ж)	[fin'ʎandija]
France	**Франция** (ж)	[fʲrantsɪja]
Sweden	**Швеция** (ж)	[ʃ'wetsɪja]

Switzerland	**Швейцария** (ж)	[ʃwi'tsarija]
Scotland	**Шотландия** (ж)	[ʃʌt'landija]
Vatican	**Ватикан** (м)	[vɑti'kɑn]
Liechtenstein	**Лихтенштейн** (м)	[lihtɛnʃ'tɛjn]
Luxembourg	**Люксембург** (м)	[lyksem'bʊrk]

Monaco	**Монако** (с)	[mɑ'nɑkə]
Albania	**Албания** (ж)	[al'banija]
Bulgaria	**Болгария** (ж)	[bal'garija]
Hungary	**Венгрия** (ж)	['wehgrija]
Latvia	**Латвия** (ж)	['lɑtwija]

Lithuania	**Литва** (ж)	[lit'vɑ]
Poland	**Польша** (ж)	['pɔʎʃə]
Romania	**Румыния** (ж)	[rʊ'mɪnija]
Serbia	**Сербия** (ж)	['serbija]
Slovakia	**Словакия** (ж)	[slɑ'vɑkija]

Croatia	**Хорватия** (ж)	[har'vɑtija]
Czech Republic	**Чехия** (ж)	['tʃehija]
Estonia	**Эстония** (ж)	[ɛs'tɔnija]
Bosnia and Herzegovina	**Босния и Герцеговина** (ж)	['bɔsnia i girtsəgɑ'winə]
Macedonia (Republic of ~)	**Македония** (ж)	[mɑke'dɔnija]

Slovenia	**Словения** (ж)	[slɑ'wenija]
Montenegro	**Черногория** (ж)	[tʃirnɑ'gɔrija]
Belarus	**Беларусь** (ж)	[bilɑ'rʊsʲ]
Moldova, Moldavia	**Молдова** (ж)	[mɑl'dɔvə]
Russia	**Россия** (ж)	[rɑ'sija]
Ukraine	**Украина** (ж)	[ukrɑ'inə]

20. Countries of the world. Part 2

Asia	**Азия** (ж)	['azija]
Vietnam	**Вьетнам** (м)	[vjet'nɑm]
India	**Индия** (ж)	['indija]
Israel	**Израиль** (м)	[iz'rɑiʎ]
China	**Китай** (м)	[ki'tɑj]

Lebanon	**Ливан** (м)	[li'vɑn]
Mongolia	**Монголия** (ж)	[mɑ'ŋɔlija]
Malaysia	**Малайзия** (ж)	[mɑ'lajzija]
Pakistan	**Пакистан** (м)	[pɑkis'tɑn]
Saudi Arabia	**Саудовская Аравия** (ж)	[sɑ'udɑfskɑja ɑ'rawija]

Thailand	Таиланд (м)	[tai'lant]
Taiwan	Тайвань (м)	[taj'vaɲ]
Turkey	Турция (ж)	['tʊrtsija]
Japan	Япония (ж)	[ja'pɔnija]
Afghanistan	Афганистан (м)	[afganis'tan]
Bangladesh	Бангладеш (м)	[bahgla'deʃ]
Indonesia	Индонезия (ж)	[inda'nɛzija]
Jordan	Иордания (ж)	[iar'danija]
Iraq	Ирак (м)	[i'rak]
Iran	Иран (м)	[i'ran]
Cambodia	Камбоджа (ж)	[kam'bɔdʒə]
Kuwait	Кувейт (м)	[kʊ'wejt]
Laos	Лаос (м)	[la'ɔs]
Myanmar	Мьянма (ж)	['mjanmə]
Nepal	Непал (м)	[ni'pal]
United Arab Emirates	Объединённые Арабские Эмираты (мн)	[abjedi'nɔnnɪe a'rapskie ɛmi'ratɪ]
Syria	Сирия (ж)	['sirija]
Palestine	Палестина (ж)	[pales'tinə]
South Korea	Южная Корея (ж)	['juʒnaja ka'reja]
North Korea	Северная Корея (ж)	['sewernaja ka'reja]
United States of America	Соединённые Штаты (мн) Америки	[saedi'nɔnnɪe ʃ'tatɪ a'meriki]
Canada	Канада (ж)	[ka'nadə]
Mexico	Мексика (ж)	['meksikə]
Argentina	Аргентина (ж)	[argen'tinə]
Brazil	Бразилия (ж)	[bra'zilija]
Colombia	Колумбия (ж)	[ka'lumbija]
Cuba	Куба (ж)	['kʊbə]
Chile	Чили (ж)	['tʃili]
Venezuela	Венесуэла (ж)	[winesʊ'ɛlə]
Ecuador	Эквадор (м)	[ɛkva'dɔr]
The Bahamas	Багамские острова (ж)	[ba'gamskie astra'va]
Panama	Панама (ж)	[pa'namə]
Egypt	Египет (м)	[e'gipet]
Morocco	Марокко (с)	[ma'rɔkkə]
Tunisia	Тунис (м)	[tʊ'nis]
Kenya	Кения (ж)	['kenija]
Libya	Ливия (ж)	['liwija]
South Africa	ЮАР (м)	[ju'ar]
Australia	Австралия (ж)	[afst'ralija]
New Zealand	Новая Зеландия (ж)	['nɔvaja ze'landija]

21. Weather. Natural disasters

weather	погода (ж)	[pa'godə]
weather forecast	прогноз (м) погоды	[prag'nos pa'godɪ]
temperature	температура (ж)	[timpera'turə]
thermometer	термометр (м)	[tir'mɔmetr]
barometer	барометр (м)	[ba'rɔmetr]
sun	солнце (с)	['sɔnʦe]
to shine (vi)	светить	[swi'tit']
sunny (day)	солнечный	['sɔlniʧnɪj]
to come up (vi)	взойти	[vzaj'ti]
to set (vi)	сесть	[sest']
rain	дождь (м)	[dɔʒt']
it's raining	идёт дождь	[i'dɜt 'dɔʒt']
pouring rain	проливной дождь (м)	[praliv'nɔj dɔʒt']
rain cloud	туча (ж)	['tuʧə]
puddle	лужа (ж)	['luʒə]
to get wet (in rain)	промокнуть	[pra'mɔknut']
thunderstorm	гроза (ж)	[gra'za]
lightning (~ strike)	молния (ж)	['mɔlnija]
to flash (vi)	сверкать	[swir'kat']
thunder	гром (м)	[grɔm]
it's thundering	гремит гром	[gri'mit grɔm]
hail	град (м)	[grat]
it's hailing	идёт град	[i'dɜt g'rat]
heat (extreme ~)	жара (ж)	[ʒa'ra]
it's hot	жарко	['ʒarkə]
it's warm	тепло	[tip'lɔ]
it's cold	холодно	['hɔladnə]
fog (mist)	туман (м)	[tu'man]
foggy	туманный	[tu'mannɪj]
cloud	облако (с)	['ɔblakə]
cloudy (adj)	облачный	['ɔblaʧnɪj]
humidity	влажность (ж)	[v'laʒnast']
snow	снег (м)	[snek]
it's snowing	идёт снег	[i'dɜt s'nek]
frost (severe ~, freezing cold)	мороз (м)	[ma'rɔs]
below zero (adv)	ниже нуля	['niʒɛ nu'ʎa]
hoarfrost	иней (м)	['inej]
bad weather	непогода (ж)	[nipa'godə]
disaster	катастрофа (ж)	[katast'rɔfə]
flood, inundation	наводнение (с)	[navad'nenie]
avalanche	лавина (ж)	[la'winə]

earthquake	землетрясение (с)	[zemletri'senie]
tremor, quake	толчок (м)	[tal'tʃɔk]
epicenter	эпицентр (м)	[ɛpi'tsentr]
eruption	извержение (с)	[izwer'ʒɛnie]
lava	лава (ж)	['lavə]
tornado	торнадо (м)	[tar'nadə]
twister	смерч (м)	[smertʃ]
hurricane	ураган (м)	[ura'gan]
tsunami	цунами (с)	[tsu'nami]
cyclone	циклон (м)	[tsik'lɔn]

22. Animals. Part 1

animal	животное (с)	[ʒı'vɔtnae]
predator	хищник (м)	['hiçnik]
tiger	тигр (м)	[tigr]
lion	лев (м)	[lef]
wolf	волк (м)	[vɔlk]
fox	лиса (ж)	['lisə]
jaguar	ягуар (м)	[jagu'ar]
lynx	рысь (ж)	[rısʲ]
coyote	койот (м)	[ka'jot]
jackal	шакал (м)	[ʃʌ'kal]
hyena	гиена (ж)	[gi'enə]
squirrel	белка (ж)	['belkə]
hedgehog	ёж (м)	[ʒʃ]
rabbit	кролик (м)	[k'rɔlik]
raccoon	енот (м)	[e'nɔt]
hamster	хомяк (м)	[ha'mʲak]
mole	крот (м)	[krɔt]
mouse	мышь (ж)	[mıʃ]
rat	крыса (ж)	[k'rısə]
bat	летучая мышь (ж)	[le'tutʃija mıʃ]
beaver	бобр (м)	[bɔbr]
horse	лошадь (ж)	['lɔʃʌtʲ]
deer	олень (м)	[a'lenʲ]
camel	верблюд (м)	[wirb'lyt]
zebra	зебра (ж)	['zebrə]
whale	кит (м)	[kit]
seal	тюлень (м)	[ty'lɛɲ]
walrus	морж (м)	[mɔrʃ]
dolphin	дельфин (м)	[diʌ'fin]
bear	медведь (м)	[mid'wetʲ]

monkey	обезьяна (ж)	[abi'zjanə]
elephant	слон (м)	[slɔn]
rhinoceros	носорог (м)	[nasa'rɔk]
giraffe	жираф (м)	[ʒɪ'raf]

hippopotamus	бегемот (м)	[bige'mɔt]
kangaroo	кенгуру (м)	[kihgu'rʊ]
cat	кошка (ж)	['kɔʃkə]

cow	корова (ж)	[ka'rɔvə]
bull	бык (м)	[bɪk]
sheep (ewe)	овца (ж)	[av'tsa]
goat	коза (ж)	[ka'za]

donkey	осёл (м)	[a'sɜl]
pig, hog	свинья (ж)	[swi'nja]
hen (chicken)	курица (ж)	['kʊritsə]
rooster	петух (м)	[pi'tʊh]

duck	утка (ж)	['utkə]
goose	гусь (м)	[gʊsʲ]
turkey (hen)	индюшка (ж)	[in'dyʃkə]
sheepdog	овчарка (ж)	[af'tʃarkə]

23. Animals. Part 2

bird	птица (ж)	[p'titsə]
pigeon	голубь (м)	['gɔlupʲ]
sparrow	воробей (м)	[vara'bej]
tit	синица (ж)	[si'nitsə]
magpie	сорока (ж)	[sa'rɔkə]

eagle	орёл (м)	[a'rɜl]
hawk	ястреб (м)	['jastrep]
falcon	сокол (м)	['sɔkal]

swan	лебедь (м)	['lebetʲ]
crane	журавль (м)	[ʒu'ravʎ]
stork	аист (м)	['aist]
parrot	попугай (м)	[papʊ'gaj]
peacock	павлин (м)	[pav'lin]
ostrich	страус (м)	[st'raus]

heron	цапля (ж)	['tsapʎa]
nightingale	соловей (м)	[sala'wej]
swallow	ласточка (ж)	['lastatʃkə]
woodpecker	дятел (м)	['dʲatel]
cuckoo	кукушка (ж)	[kʊ'kuʃkə]
owl	сова (ж)	[sa'va]
penguin	пингвин (м)	[pihg'win]

tuna	тунец (м)	[tʊˈnets]
trout	форель (ж)	[faˈreʎ]
eel	угорь (м)	[ˈugarʲ]

shark	акула (ж)	[aˈkʊlə]
crab	краб (м)	[krap]
jellyfish	медуза (ж)	[miˈdʊzə]
octopus	осьминог (м)	[asʲmiˈnɔk]

starfish	морская звезда (ж)	[marsˈkaja zwezˈda]
sea urchin	морской ёж (м)	[marsˈkɔj ʒʃ]
seahorse	морской конёк (м)	[marsˈkɔj kaˈnɜk]
shrimp	креветка (ж)	[kriˈwetkə]

snake	змея (ж)	[zmiˈja]
viper	гадюка (ж)	[gaˈdykə]
lizard	ящерица (ж)	[ˈjaɕiritsə]
iguana	игуана (ж)	[igʊˈanə]
chameleon	хамелеон (м)	[hamiliˈɔn]
scorpion	скорпион (м)	[skarpiˈɔn]

turtle	черепаха (ж)	[ʧiriˈpahə]
frog	лягушка (ж)	[liˈgʊʃkə]
crocodile	крокодил (м)	[krakaˈdil]

insect, bug	насекомое (с)	[naseˈkɔmae]
butterfly	бабочка (ж)	[ˈbabaʧkə]
ant	муравей (м)	[mʊraˈwej]
fly	муха (ж)	[ˈmʊhə]

mosquito	комар (м)	[kaˈmar]
beetle	жук (м)	[ʒuk]
bee	пчела (ж)	[pʧiˈla]
spider	паук (м)	[paˈuk]

24. Trees. Plants

tree	дерево (с)	[ˈderevə]
birch	берёза (ж)	[biˈrɜzə]
oak	дуб (м)	[dʊp]
linden tree	липа (ж)	[ˈlipə]
aspen	осина (ж)	[aˈsinə]

maple	клён (м)	[ˈklɜn]
spruce	ель (ж)	[eʎ]
pine	сосна (ж)	[sasˈna]
cedar	кедр (м)	[kedr]

| poplar | тополь (м) | [ˈtɔpaʎ] |
| rowan | рябина (ж) | [riˈbinə] |

beech	бук (м)	[bʊk]
elm	вяз (м)	[vʲas]
ash (tree)	ясень (м)	['jaseɲ]
chestnut	каштан (м)	[kaʃ'tan]
palm tree	пальма (ж)	['paʎmə]
bush	куст (м)	[kʊst]
mushroom	гриб (м)	[grip]
poisonous mushroom	ядовитый гриб (м)	[jada'witɪj grip]
cep (Boletus edulis)	белый гриб (м)	['belɪj grip]
russula	сыроежка (ж)	[sɪra'eʃkə]
fly agaric	мухомор (м)	[mʊha'mɔr]
death cap	поганка (ж)	[pa'gankə]
flower	цветок (м)	[ʦwi'tɔk]
bouquet (of flowers)	букет (м)	[bʊ'ket]
rose (flower)	роза (ж)	['rɔzə]
tulip	тюльпан (м)	[tyʎ'pɑn]
carnation	гвоздика (ж)	[gvaz'dikə]
camomile	ромашка (ж)	[ra'maʃkə]
cactus	кактус (м)	['kaktʊs]
lily of the valley	ландыш (м)	['landɪʃ]
snowdrop	подснежник (м)	[pats'neʒnik]
water lily	кувшинка (ж)	[kʊf'ʃinkə]
greenhouse (tropical ~)	оранжерея (ж)	[aranʒɪ'reja]
lawn	газон (м)	[ga'zɔn]
flowerbed	клумба (ж)	[k'lumbə]
plant	растение (с)	[ras'tenie]
grass	трава (ж)	[tra'va]
leaf	лист (м)	[list]
petal	лепесток (м)	[lipes'tɔk]
stem	стебель (м)	[s'tebeʎ]
young plant (shoot)	росток (м)	[ras'tɔk]
cereal crops	зерновые растения (с мн)	[zerna'vie ras'tenija]
wheat	пшеница (ж)	[pʃɪ'nitsə]
rye	рожь (ж)	[rɔʃ]
oats	овёс (м)	[a'wɜs]
millet	просо (с)	[p'rɔsə]
barley	ячмень (м)	[itʃ'meɲ]
corn	кукуруза (ж)	[kʊkʊ'rʊzə]
rice	рис (м)	[ris]

25. Various useful words

balance (of situation)	**баланс** (м)	[ba'lans]
base (basis)	**база** (ж)	['bazə]
beginning	**начало** (с)	[na'tʃalə]
category	**категория** (ж)	[kate'gɔrija]
choice	**выбор** (м)	['vɪbar]
coincidence	**совпадение** (с)	[safpa'denie]
comparison	**сравнение** (с)	[srav'nenie]
degree (extent, amount)	**степень** (ж)	[s'tepeɲ]
development	**развитие** (с)	[raz'witie]
difference	**различие** (с)	[raz'litʃie]
effect (e.g., of drugs)	**эффект** (м)	[ɛ'fekt]
effort (exertion)	**усилие** (с)	[u'silie]
element	**элемент** (м)	[ɛli'ment]
example (illustration)	**пример** (м)	[pri'mer]
fact	**факт** (м)	[fakt]
help	**помощь** (ж)	['pɔmaɕ]
ideal	**идеал** (м)	[idi'al]
kind (sort, type)	**вид** (м)	[wit]
mistake, error	**ошибка** (ж)	[a'ʃipkə]
moment	**момент** (м)	[ma'ment]
obstacle	**препятствие** (с)	[pri'pʲatstwie]
part (~ of sth)	**часть** (ж)	[tʃastʲ]
pause (break)	**пауза** (ж)	['pauzə]
position	**позиция** (ж)	[pa'zitsɪja]
problem	**проблема** (ж)	[prab'lemə]
process	**процесс** (м)	[pra'tses]
progress	**прогресс** (м)	[prag'rɛs]
property (quality)	**свойство** (с)	[s'vɔjstvə]
reaction	**реакция** (ж)	[ri'aktsɪja]
risk	**риск** (м)	[risk]
secret	**тайна** (ж)	['tajnə]
series	**серия** (ж)	['serija]
shape (outer form)	**форма** (ж)	['fɔrmə]
situation	**ситуация** (ж)	[situ'atsɪja]
solution	**решение** (с)	[ri'ʃenie]
standard (adj)	**стандартный**	[stan'dartnɪj]
stop (pause)	**остановка** (ж)	[asta'nɔfkə]
style	**стиль** (м)	[stiʎ]
system	**система** (ж)	[sis'temə]

| table (chart) | таблица (ж) | [tab'litsə] |
| tempo, rate | темп (м) | [tɛmp] |

term (word, expression)	термин (м)	['termin]
truth (e.g., moment of ~)	истина (ж)	['istinə]
turn (please wait your ~)	очередь (ж)	['ɔtʃiretʲ]
urgent (adj)	срочный	[s'rɔtʃnij]

utility (usefulness)	польза (ж)	['pɔʎzə]
variant (alternative)	вариант (м)	[vari'ant]
way (means, method)	способ (м)	[s'pɔsap]
zone	зона (ж)	['zɔnə]

26. Modifiers. Adjectives. Part 1

additional (adj)	дополнительный	[dapal'niteʎnij]
ancient (~ civilization)	древний	[d'revnij]
artificial (adj)	искусственный	[is'kustwennij]
bad (adj)	плохой	[pla'hɔj]
beautiful (person)	красивый	[kra'sivij]

big (in size)	большой	[baʎ'ʃɔj]
bitter (taste)	горький	['gɔrʲkij]
blind (sightless)	слепой	[sli'pɔj]
central (adj)	центральный	[tsint'raʎnij]

children's (adj)	детский	['detskij]
clandestine (secret)	подпольный	[pat'pɔʎnij]
clean (free from dirt)	чистый	['tʃistij]
clever (smart)	умный	['umnij]
compatible (adj)	совместимый	[savmes'timij]

contented (satisfied)	довольный	[da'vɔʎnij]
dangerous (adj)	опасный	[a'pasnij]
dead (not alive)	мёртвый	['mɜrtvij]
dense (fog, smoke)	плотный	[p'lɔtnij]
difficult (decision)	трудный	[t'rudnij]

dirty (not clean)	грязный	[g'rʲaznij]
easy (not difficult)	лёгкий	['lɜhkij]
empty (glass, room)	пустой	[pus'tɔj]
exact (amount)	точный	['tɔtʃnij]
excellent (adj)	отличный	[at'litʃnij]

excessive (adj)	чрезмерный	[tʃrez'mernij]
exterior (adj)	внешний	[v'neʃnij]
fast (quick)	быстрый	['bistrij]
fertile (land, soil)	плодородный	[plada'rɔdnij]
fragile (china, glass)	хрупкий	[h'rupkij]
free (at no cost)	бесплатный	[bisp'latnij]

fresh (~ water)	пресный	[p'resnɪj]
frozen (food)	замороженный	[zamʌ'rɔʒɪnɪj]
full (completely filled)	полный	['pɔlnɪj]
happy (adj)	счастливый	[ɕis'livɪj]
hard (not soft)	твёрдый	['twɜrdɪj]
huge (adj)	огромный	[ag'rɔmnɪj]
ill (sick, unwell)	больной	[baʎ'nɔj]
immobile (adj)	неподвижный	[nɪpad'wɪʒnɪj]
important (adj)	важный	['vaʒnɪj]
interior (adj)	внутренний	[v'nʊtrenɪj]
last (e.g., ~ week)	прошлый	[p'rɔʃlɪj]
last (final)	последний	[pas'lednɪj]
left (e.g., ~ side)	левый	['levɪj]
legal (legitimate)	законный	[zaʾkɔnnɪj]
light (in weight)	лёгкий	['lɜɦkij]
liquid (fluid)	жидкий	['ʒitkij]
long (e.g., ~ hair)	длинный	[d'linnɪj]
loud (voice, etc.)	громкий	[g'rɔmkij]
low (voice)	тихий	['tihij]

27. Modifiers. Adjectives. Part 2

main (principal)	главный	[g'lavnɪj]
matt, matte	матовый	['matavɪj]
mysterious (adj)	загадочный	[zaʾgadatʃnɪj]
narrow (street, etc.)	узкий	['uskij]
native (~ country)	родной	[rad'nɔj]
negative (~ response)	отрицательный	[atri'tsateʎnɪj]
new (adj)	новый	['nɔvɪj]
next (e.g., ~ week)	следующий	[s'ledʊɕij]
normal (adj)	нормальный	[nar'maʎnɪj]
not difficult (adj)	нетрудный	[nit'rʊdnɪj]
obligatory (adj)	обязательный	[abi'zateʎnɪj]
old (house)	старый	[s'tarɪj]
open (adj)	открытый	[atk'rɪtɪj]
opposite (adj)	противоположный	[prativapaʾlɔʒnɪj]
ordinary (usual)	обыкновенный	[abɪknaʾwennɪj]
original (unusual)	оригинальный	[arigi'naʎnɪj]
personal (adj)	персональный	[pirsaʾnaʎnɪj]
polite (adj)	вежливый	['weʒlivɪj]
poor (not rich)	бедный	['bednɪj]
possible (adj)	возможный	[vaz'mɔʒnɪj]
principal (main)	основной	[asnav'nɔj]

probable (adj)	вероятный	[wirʌ'jatnɪj]
prolonged (e.g., ~ applause)	продолжительный	[prɑdɑ'ʒiteʎnɪj]
public (open to all)	общественный	[ɑp'ɕestwenɪj]
rare (adj)	редкий	['retkij]
raw (uncooked)	сырой	[sɪ'rɔj]
right (not left)	правый	[p'rɑvɪj]
ripe (fruit)	зрелый	[z'relɪj]
risky (adj)	рискованный	[ris'kɔvɑnɪj]
sad (~ look)	печальный	[pi'ʧaʎnɪj]
second hand (adj)	бывший в употреблении	['bɪfʃɪj v upɑtreb'lenii]
shallow (water)	мелкий	['melkij]
sharp (blade, etc.)	острый	['ɔstrɪj]
short (in length)	короткий	[kɑ'rɔtkij]
similar (adj)	похожий	[pɑ'hɔʒɪj]
smooth (surface)	гладкий	[g'lɑtkij]
soft (~ toys)	мягкий	['mʲaɦkij]
solid (~ wall)	прочный	[p'rɔʧnɪj]
sour (flavor, taste)	кислый	['kislɪj]
spacious (house, etc.)	просторный	[prɑs'tɔrnɪj]
special (adj)	специальный	[spitsɪ'aʎnɪj]
straight (line, road)	прямой	[pri'mɔj]
strong (person)	сильный	['siʎnɪj]
stupid (foolish)	глупый	[g'lupɪj]
superb, perfect (adj)	превосходный	[privɑs'hɔdnɪj]
sweet (sugary)	сладкий	[s'lɑtkij]
tan (adj)	загорелый	[zɑgɑ'relɪj]
tasty (delicious)	вкусный	[f'kʊsnɪj]
unclear (adj)	неясный	[ni'jasnɪj]

28. Verbs. Part 1

to accuse (vt)	обвинять	[ɑbwi'ɲatʲ]
to agree (say yes)	соглашаться	[sɑglɑ'ʃʌtsə]
to announce (vt)	объявлять	[ɑbʰiv'ʎatʲ]
to answer (vi, vt)	отвечать	[ɑtwe'ʧatʲ]
to apologize (vi)	извиняться	[izwi'ɲatsə]
to arrive (vi)	приезжать	[prii'zatʲ]
to ask (~ oneself)	спрашивать	[sp'rɑʃivatʲ]
to be absent	отсутствовать	[ɑ'tsutstvɑvatʲ]
to be afraid	бояться	[bɑ'jatsə]
to be born	родиться	[rɑ'ditsə]

to be in a hurry	спешить	[spi'ʃitʲ]
to beat (to hit)	бить	[bitʲ]
to begin (vt)	начинать	[nɑtʃi'natʲ]
to believe (in God)	верить	['weritʲ]
to belong to …	принадлежать …	[prinadle'ʒatʲ]
to break (split into pieces)	ломать	[la'matʲ]
to build (vt)	строить	[st'rɔitʲ]
to buy (purchase)	покупать	[paku'patʲ]
can (v aux)	мочь	[mɔtʃ]
can (v aux)	мочь	[mɔtʃ]
to cancel (call off)	отменить	[atme'nitʲ]
to catch (vt)	ловить	[la'witʲ]
to change (vt)	изменить	[izme'nitʲ]
to check (to examine)	проверять	[prawe'rʲatʲ]
to choose (select)	выбирать	[vɪbi'ratʲ]
to clean up (tidy)	убирать	[ubi'ratʲ]
to close (vt)	закрывать	[zakrɪ'vatʲ]
to compare (vt)	сравнивать	[s'ravnivatʲ]
to complain (vi, vt)	жаловаться	['ʒalavatsə]
to confirm (vt)	подтвердить	[patwer'ditʲ]
to congratulate (vt)	поздравлять	[pazdrav'ʎatʲ]
to cook (dinner)	готовить	[ga'tɔwitʲ]
to copy (vt)	скопировать	[ska'piravatʲ]
to cost (vt)	стоить	[s'tɔitʲ]
to count (add up)	считать	[ɕi'tatʲ]
to count on …	рассчитывать на …	[ra'ɕitɪvatʲ na]
to create (vt)	создать	[saz'datʲ]
to cry (weep)	плакать	[p'lakatʲ]
to dance (vi, vt)	танцевать	[tantsɪ'vatʲ]
to deceive (vi, vt)	обманывать	[ab'manɪvatʲ]
to decide (~ to do sth)	решать	[ri'ʃʌtʲ]
to delete (vt)	удалить	[uda'litʲ]
to demand (request firmly)	требовать	[t'rebavatʲ]
to deny (vt)	отрицать	[atri'tsatʲ]
to depend on …	зависеть	[za'wisetʲ]
to despise (vt)	презирать	[prizi'ratʲ]
to die (vi)	умереть	[umi'retʲ]
to dig (vt)	рыть	[rɪtʲ]
to disappear (vi)	исчезнуть	[i'ɕeznʊtʲ]
to discuss (vt)	обсуждать	[apsʊʒ'datʲ]
to disturb (vt)	беспокоить	[bispa'kɔitʲ]

29. Verbs. Part 2

to dive (vi)	нырять	[nɪˈrʲatʲ]
to divorce (vi)	развестись	[razwesˈtisʲ]
to do (vt)	делать	[ˈdelatʲ]
to doubt (have doubts)	сомневаться	[samniˈvatsə]
to drink (vi, vt)	пить	[pitʲ]
to drop (let fall)	ронять	[raˈɲatʲ]
to dry (clothes, hair)	сушить	[sʊˈʃitʲ]
to eat (vi, vt)	есть	[estʲ]
to end (~ a relationship)	прекращать	[prikraˈɕatʲ]
to excuse (forgive)	извинять	[izwiˈɲatʲ]
to exist (vi)	существовать	[sʊɕestvaˈvatʲ]
to expect (foresee)	предвидеть	[pridˈwidetʲ]
to explain (vt)	объяснять	[abʰesˈɲatʲ]
to fall (vi)	падать	[ˈpadatʲ]
to fight (street fight, etc.)	драться	[dˈratsə]
to find (vt)	находить	[nahaˈditʲ]
to finish (vt)	заканчивать	[zaˈkaɲtʃivatʲ]
to fly (vi)	лететь	[liˈtetʲ]
to forbid (vt)	запретить	[zapriˈtitʲ]
to forget (vi, vt)	забывать	[zabɪˈvatʲ]
to forgive (vt)	прощать	[praˈɕatʲ]
to get tired	уставать	[ustaˈvatʲ]
to give (vt)	давать	[daˈvatʲ]
to go (on foot)	идти	[itʲˈti]
to hate (vt)	ненавидеть	[ninaˈwidetʲ]
to have (vt)	иметь	[iˈmetʲ]
to have breakfast	завтракать	[ˈzaftrakatʲ]
to have dinner	ужинать	[ˈuʒɪnatʲ]
to have lunch	обедать	[aˈbedatʲ]
to hear (vt)	слышать	[sˈlɪʃʌtʲ]
to help (vt)	помогать	[pamaˈgatʲ]
to hide (vt)	прятать	[pˈrʲatatʲ]
to hope (vi, vt)	надеяться	[naˈdeitsə]
to hunt (vi, vt)	охотиться	[aˈhotitsə]
to hurry (vi)	торопиться	[taraˈpitsə]
to insist (vi, vt)	настаивать	[nasˈtaivatʲ]
to insult (vt)	оскорблять	[askarbˈʎatʲ]
to invite (vt)	приглашать	[priglaˈʃʌtʲ]
to joke (vi)	шутить	[ʃʊˈtitʲ]
to keep (vt)	сохранять	[sahraˈɲatʲ]
to kill (vt)	убивать	[ubiˈvatʲ]
to know (sb)	знать	[znatʲ]

to like (I like ...)	нравиться	[n'rawitsə]
to look at ...	глядеть на ...	[gli'detʲ na]
to lose (umbrella, etc.)	терять	[ti'rʲatʲ]
to love (sb)	любить	[lʲu'bitʲ]
to make a mistake	ошибаться	[aʃɨ'batsə]
to meet (vi, vt)	встречаться	[fstre'tʃatsə]
to miss (school, etc.)	пропускать	[prapʊs'katʲ]

30. Verbs. Part 3

to obey (vi, vt)	подчиниться	[patʃi'nitsə]
to open (vt)	открывать	[atkrɨ'vatʲ]
to participate (vi)	участвовать	[u'tʃastvavatʲ]
to pay (vi, vt)	платить	[pla'titʲ]
to permit (vt)	разрешать	[razre'ʃʌtʲ]
to play (children)	играть	[ig'ratʲ]
to pray (vi, vt)	молиться	[ma'litsə]
to promise (vt)	обещать	[abi'ɕatʲ]
to propose (vt)	предлагать	[pridla'gatʲ]
to prove (vt)	доказывать	[da'kazɨvatʲ]
to read (vi, vt)	читать	[tʃi'tatʲ]
to receive (vt)	получить	[palu'tʃitʲ]
to rent (sth from sb)	снимать	[sni'matʲ]
to repeat (say again)	повторять	[pafta'rʲatʲ]
to reserve, to book	резервировать	[rezir'wiravatʲ]
to run (vi)	бежать	[bi'ʒatʲ]
to save (rescue)	спасать	[spa'satʲ]
to say (~ thank you)	сказать	[ska'zatʲ]
to see (vt)	видеть	['widetʲ]
to sell (vt)	продавать	[prada'vatʲ]
to send (vt)	отправлять	[atprav'ʎatʲ]
to shoot (vi)	стрелять	[stri'ʎatʲ]
to shout (vi)	кричать	[kri'tʃatʲ]
to show (vt)	показывать	[pa'kazɨvatʲ]
to sign (document)	подписывать	[pat'pisɨvatʲ]
to sing (vi)	петь	[petʲ]
to sit down (vi)	садиться	[sa'ditsə]
to smile (vi)	улыбаться	[ulɨ'batsə]
to speak (vi, vt)	говорить	[gava'ritʲ]
to steal (money, etc.)	красть	[krastʲ]
to stop (please ~ calling me)	прекращать	[prikra'ɕatʲ]
to study (vt)	изучать	[izu'tʃatʲ]
to swim (vi)	плавать	[p'lavatʲ]

to take (vt)	брать	[bratʲ]
to talk to …	говорить с …	[gavaˈritʲ s]
to tell (story, joke)	рассказывать	[rasˈkazıvatʲ]
to thank (vt)	благодарить	[blagadaˈritʲ]
to think (vi, vt)	думать	[ˈdʊmatʲ]

to translate (vt)	переводить	[pirevaˈditʲ]
to trust (vt)	доверять	[daweˈrʲatʲ]
to try (attempt)	пытаться	[pıˈtatsə]
to turn (e.g., ~ left)	поворачивать	[pavaˈratʃivatʲ]
to turn off	выключать	[vıklyˈtʃatʲ]

to turn on	включать	[fklyˈtʃatʲ]
to understand (vt)	понимать	[paniˈmatʲ]
to wait (vt)	ждать	[ʒdatʲ]
to want (wish, desire)	хотеть	[haˈtetʲ]
to work (vi)	работать	[raˈbotatʲ]
to write (vt)	писать	[piˈsatʲ]

www.ingramcontent.com/pod-product-compliance
Lightning Source LLC
Chambersburg PA
CBHW060026050426
42448CB00012B/2876